# ANNE MORRIN

## The Ireland We Remember

Trafford
PUBLISHING

Order this book online at www.trafford.com/08-0852
or email orders@trafford.com

Most Trafford titles are also available at major online book retailers.

© Copyright 2008 Anne Morrin.
Illustrated by Claire Morrin.
Cover Design/Artwork by Claire Morrin.
All rights reserved. No part of this publication may be reproduced, stored in a retrieval system, or transmitted, in any form or by any means, electronic, mechanical, photocopying, recording, or otherwise, without the written prior permission of the author.

Note for Librarians: A cataloguing record for this book is available from Library and Archives Canada at www.collectionscanada.ca/amicus/index-e.html

Printed in Victoria, BC, Canada.

ISBN: 978-1-4251-8194-9

*We at Trafford believe that it is the responsibility of us all, as both individuals and corporations, to make choices that are environmentally and socially sound. You, in turn, are supporting this responsible conduct each time you purchase a Trafford book, or make use of our publishing services. To find out how you are helping, please visit www.trafford.com/responsiblepublishing.html*

*Our mission is to efficiently provide the world's finest, most comprehensive book publishing service, enabling every author to experience success. To find out how to publish your book, your way, and have it available worldwide, visit us online at www.trafford.com/10510*

**Trafford**
PUBLISHING   www.trafford.com

**North America & international**
toll-free: 1 888 232 4444 (USA & Canada)
phone: 250 383 6864 ♦ fax: 250 383 6804 ♦ email: info@trafford.com

**The United Kingdom & Europe**
phone: +44 (0)1865 487 395 ♦ local rate: 0845 230 9601
facsimile: +44 (0)1865 481 507 ♦ email: info.uk@trafford.com

10 9 8 7 6 5 4 3 2

CHAPTER 1

# The Terrible Twins

JUDY'S IMAGE OF GRANDMOTHERS was not very flattering. In her seven year old mind she saw them as 'Red Riding Hood Grannies', with black shawl, heavy cane, toothless grin and reading glasses perched on top of their noses. Therefore, it was with some misgiving that she now scrutinized her own grandmother who came to take care of the family while Mum went away to bring home another baby.

Grandmother was not old, nor did she wear a shawl, or even remotely resemble 'Granny in the Woods.' Judy stared now at her greying hair, and thought sulkily, "Why can't she put her hair in a 'bun', like the 'other granny'?" Her young eyes roamed over Grandmother's smart navy outfit which she was well aware would be exchanged for more comfortable working clothes immediately on arrival at the farm.

Judy could not quite figure out why Grandmother was holding her hankie to her nose as she got out of the car and why Dad was roaring with laughter, suggesting that next time he would remember to bring a gas mask. Later on,

Judy realised that Grandmother was vigorously objecting to the 'pong' inside the car. Dad referred to it as a 'hum' and it never particularly worried him. He put sheep in the boot, and Tramp his faithful collie dog, usually settled himself comfortably in the back seat. Wherever his master went, he went also.

The children softened toffee on the dashboard, in the strong sunshine, and kept an ample supply of chewing gum stuck to the rear of the driver and passenger seats. Grandmother was adamant in her refusal to sit into that 'smelly heap' again, and equipped for any eventuality she donned her oilskins and wellies first thing next morning, to disinfect and scrub the car until her arms ached. She would have something to say to the first child who brought toffee or gum into that car again. Tramp sniffed scornfully and padded away, while the children chorused,

"We got a brand new car today!"

The new babies invariably arrived during summer school holidays each year. Judy loved the warm cuddly newcomers, with their soft skin, and 'powdery' smell, but she told herself she certainly didn't love her grandmother, who always insisted that the eight little Mannion children tidy up the kitchen each morning, and horror of horrors, help to tidy up their bedrooms also. Mum never minded that the place looked like a bomb-site, but Grandmother was forever mopping and dusting.

"Why doesn't she get old and wrinkly?" Judy said unkindly to her twin brother Johnny.

Unconsciously, they became two very rebellious children, who needed a firm hand to guide them. This was a very delicate situation for Grandmother who lectured them firmly each day on their despicable manners, especially at table. Meal times were 'trying' to say the least, and while those two little terrors admitted grudgingly that Grandmother produced 'nice dinners', they resented the fact that there was 'one menu only'. Mum always allowed them to pick and choose, but now they must eat what was served or go hungry. No nonsense.

With each passing year, Grandmother understood more clearly the reasons for her daughter's wan looks, her extreme fatigue and her lack of interest in parenting. It was practically impossible to cope with meals, their mother confided. One child demanded 'pale' chips and sausages, while another screamed for 'brown' chips and burgers, and five of them 'snacked' on crisps and coke in bed each night. Mollie, their mother, and Joe, their father, seemed to think this was 'just a phase'.

"Ten years on, they won't give a hoot about crisps," Joe would say, offhand, and go back to his cows and sheep.

Grandmother disagreed privately. She loved her grandchildren, but their appalling lack of discipline disturbed her. She suspected her daughter was too tired to correct them anymore. With another baby each year, she seemed to have less time for the older ones. The twins, in particular, were confused that their Mum no longer took the time to sit with them in the evenings or sing for them as she had done in earlier years.

"Mum's voice is beautiful," Judy used to think, as she sat on the rug and gazed up at her in admiration.

Mum and Dad lived on a farm in County Galway, where they kept cows and sheep and hens, while Grandmother lived miles away in Limerick city. Having lived on a farm all her life it was wonderful to get away from the traffic and the crowds in summer. She would slip into the role of housekeeper/farmhand with obvious delight from the moment she arrived at the farm. The children were unaware of this.

"Gran is a city slicker," their Dad would laughingly tell them when their enquiring minds got busy.

Grandmother particularly liked to feed the hens. She would fold her arms, and look on proudly as they devoured the grain she fed from the bucket. Johnny decided it would be the ideal time to scare her. He lay behind the wall one morning, with Trigger, the cat, under his arm. With perfect timing, he slung the terrified Trigger over the wall, almost knocking Grandmother over, as hens screeched and squawked, running in all directions.

Trigger went berserk. Feathers were flying all over. A brute of a big red cock flapped his wings wildly, sending Trigger streaking up the nearest tree, spitting viciously.

Some days later, Judy and Johnny sneaked two caterpillars into Grandmother's bed, taking great care to place them where she would undoubtedly see them, on turning back the bedclothes, but Grandmother was made of stern stuff, and the shrieks which the children hoped to hear, failed to materialise. They dropped a spider in her lap when she dozed off to sleep, and even managed to find a frog on a damp evening, which left slimy patches on the kitchen floor, practically exhausting their grandmother's patience, but fortunately for her, her breaking point was extremely high.

She was well aware of their animosity, but was prepared to endure it, if only to instil a little discipline in these unruly children, with their beautiful blonde hair and innocent blue eyes. She disliked the continuous over-lapping of meal times, that the children, if they had their way, liked to indulge in. She detested the 'snap, crackle and pop' under her feet, as they helped her, unwillingly, to make beds and tidy rooms. Above all, she was acutely aware of the need for guidance and discipline in all children, but especially in the seven year old twins.

At the end of her two week stay she decided to extend her visit. Her daughter would appreciate the much needed assistance, with another baby to care for. This would provide the opportunity to mould those two imps into loving and obedient youngsters, a task which had left Grandmother exhausted and almost defeated throughout the previous two weeks.

The dismay on Judy's face was almost comical when she learned of the extended visit.

"Mum doesn't love us anymore," she told Johnny, tearfully, when she realised Grandmother would supervise the older children, while Mum took care of the new baby.

"I've seen it all before," Grandmother told her daughter, during one of the twins' tantrums, as she briskly mopped the kitchen floor.

"Human nature doesn't alter much," she added with perception.

She was determined to win them over. Underneath her stern exterior she had a big, big heart. She gave them a lot of love, mixed gently with firmness and perseverance, and moderate expectations of obedience, in the early weeks. Gradually, and with elated spirit, she achieved her goal. Judy, hesitant at first, began to 'thaw out' and actually enjoyed the loving hugs with which Grandmother rewarded her for her good behaviour. Johnny exclaimed, with manly pride, that he no longer needed crisps and coke in bed. He really liked his clean room, but was slightly embarrassed to admit it to Grandmother just yet.

Grandmother's day of triumph came, when confined to bed with severe 'flu, they picked blue-bells for the jam-jar on the kitchen window and brought them to her room. Both of them climbed onto her bed and whispered shyly,

"We love you Gran. Please get well soon. We miss you a lot."

# Anne Morrin

*The Hyper-Active Youngsters*

CHAPTER 2

# Mongan's Boy

THIRTEEN YEARS OF MY young life were spent in an industrial school in the west of Ireland. At the tender age of three, my mother died suddenly, leaving my father to cope with the upbringing of four small children. It was accepted as the norm in the thirties to send your children off to one of these institutions, if you were a father with a job outside the home. Widowed mothers, I learned later in life, tended to hold on to the children, by working as cleaners during school hours, if they happened to live in a city or town, thereby managing to scrape through the financially lean years.

I detested that school. In my early years I cried myself to sleep at night, fervently hoping that tomorrow my father would come and take me home. He never did, of course, and I was forced to reconcile myself to the fact that I would never see him again.

I lived in fear of my superiors, who seemed so cold and so cruel. They solved all problems with the cane. My dormitory mates had more 'guts' than I had, and refused to cry, regardless of the severity of the caning.

"Come on, Jimmy," they whispered urgently, "don't give them the satisfaction of seeing you cry. They'll only give you more."

The cruelty and the savagery of those people defied belief. Much better not to dwell on it. Many years later, when I married and had a little boy of my own, I vowed that never, ever would he be disciplined with a cane. There had to be another method.

An epidemic of life-taking whooping cough swept through the school when I was ten. The younger children were the unfortunate victims. In one week, five died. My superiors must have felt I would be next, as they whispered to each other and looked at me with concern. I was so thin and pale, with my dark hair continually damp against my forehead, from persistent coughing and weakness.

'Jimmy Dunne is well done' the other boys chanted with characteristic tactlessness, as I lay limply in bed, waiting to die.

Miraculously, I survived, but after the week that was in it, dying suddenly wasn't the distant possibility it had once been.

Like all the other boys at school, once I reached the age of fourteen, I waited anxiously for someone to come and take me away. People applied to their parish priest, or directly to the school, for domestic help or farmhands, and the most suitable ones were pressed into service as they came of age. There was very little money, if any, involved. Industrial boys and girls worked primarily for their food and clothes, with the odd six-pence for a very special occasion.

At sixteen, I had almost despaired of ever getting a job. Nobody seemed to require my services. Then suddenly, unexpectedly, I was told one day that I would be going to a farm in County Mayo. I was overjoyed.

"You must work very hard or you will be returned to us," my superior warned me coldly, sliding the cane through work-worn long fingers.

That night I promised God I would do ANYTHING! I would work 'till I wore the nails off my hands. "But please, dear God," I begged, "don't ever send me back in here again."

I was dispatched via the mail car to a post office some twenty miles away, where I was transferred to another mail car operating in the south Mayo area, near enough to my destination. I walked the remaining three miles to the farm, pausing occasionally to glance at the slip of paper in my pocket, which read, 'Micheal Mongan, Caherdearg' ...... my sole introduction to my new employer.

The Mongans were a childless couple. Michael Mongan was a fifty-five years old tall, thin dark-haired man. Very rough and very blustery, with a penchant for gambling and drink, while Mrs. Mongan who was fifty, was a kind and gentle lady, frail-looking, with fair hair parted at the centre, both front and back, and rolled at the ends with two pipe cleaners.

"Ye'll eat at that small table in there," Mr Mongan told me on arrival, pointing to the back-kitchen.

Almost immediately I discovered that the small table was in fact a strong wooden box, covered with a piece of oil cloth, and normally used to accommodate buckets of spring water, and also the bucket of milk, which I quickly learned to milk from the cow, morning and evening.

My bed was a makeshift wooden frame, in a corner of the barn. On this was thrown a torn mattress, with a couple of thin blankets and a feather pillow. Servant boys seldom enjoyed the luxury of sleeping in the master's house in those days, and Michael Mongan firmly believed in 'keeping with the times'.

I didn't give a toss. I was reasonably comfortable and I was free. There was no one sweeping in at midnight to slap my face if I was still awake. I could have shouted for joy. To be free of that school forever. Little did I realise that my superiors were fervently hoping that they had seen the last of me also. They usually had difficulty placing thin, pale, light-weight boys on farms, but apparently I was selected as much for housework as for the farm.

Within a week, when Mrs Mongan was confident that her husband would not check 'my bedroom' she brought me a towel and a tin basin to wash in.

"There's plenty of water in the barrel," she told me, her eyes wandering to my none-too-clean hands.

She also brought me a candle, stuck in a jam pot, urgently requesting me to hide it.

"Now, yer not to light it unless ye get a pain or somethin', d'ye hear me?" she warned, pressing a small statue of the Virgin Mary into my hand at the same time.

"Put it under the pillow with yer rosary beads, and the mice won't come near ye," she added, as she returned to her kitchen, and her lonely wait for a husband who seldom came home before dawn. I had no idea then what connection there was between a lighted candle and a pain, but I suspected afterwards that she wished me to be wretched in comfort if the occasion arose.

I worked hard and I was happy. I actually started to put on weight and if Mrs. Mongan's measuring tape was correct I was growing every day.

"Ye'll make a fine man when ye have some good feedin' inside yer shirt," she told me, with satisfaction as she folded up her tape.

This was no nine-to-five job. I was on the go from early morning until dusk crept stealthily over the village, as late as eleven o'clock in summer time. Michael Mongan put very little effort into his small farm, and as the months passed he delegated more and more of the responsibilities to me. I was extremely proud of this and worked even harder to show my appreciation.

He didn't figure largely in my life, other than to bark out orders occasionally. I ensured he never had anything to complain about. Once during the early weeks I felt the harsh, rough edge of his tongue, and once was quite sufficient.

On the numerous occasions when her husband was absent at mealtimes, Mrs. Mongan invited me to eat at her table. When I hesitated at first, she reassured me by saying,

"Ye'll keep me company and ye can tell me what yer doin' in the fields. Yer a grown up man now."

It was said so nicely, I felt I really was grown up. Then shaking her head sadly she'd whisper, "Ye shouldn't be....." and her voice would ebb away. Unswerving loyalty forbade her to say I shouldn't be eating alone in that back kitchen. I did however, notice her silence when Mr. Mongan was present. She would look at me pleadingly, as if begging for understanding, and I ate in solitude at 'the small table' with Mackeen, the black gun dog, for company.

Relief flooded through me on those occasions. I didn't have to look at Mr. Mongan's blood-shot eyes, constantly weepy at the outer corners. Nor did I have to see the crop of straggly wet hairs, crawling down from his nose, which he wiped with the back of his hand, making my stomach take up residence in my throat. The strong odour of cigarette smoke and whiskey filled the kitchen, imposing the necessity to open all doors and windows, lest his wife's stomach reacted as mine did. She, also, was relieved when he departed for the afternoon, fully aware that she had seen the last of him 'till sunrise.

Mrs. Mongan became my mother and my friend. She treated me like the son she never had. I assisted her gladly with all the housework, preferably when her husband was away, although I was loathe to admit it. I carried countless buckets of water from the village well to fill the barrels for wash day. I hung the big black pot full of water over the huge turf fire in the kitchen to heat for washing. Most weeks I washed out every item in the washtub and insisted that Mrs. Mongan put her feet up while I worked.

Once her husband put in an unexpected appearance and it angered me to see her hastily grab some previously washed shirts, flinging them into the tub whilst she busily rewashed them almost as if she feared him. Rage welled up inside me. I had difficulty restraining myself from giving him the boot where it hurt as I watched the sneer on his face. I fought it with deep hard breaths, clinging desperately to a thin edge of control. I felt like a grown up son ready to protect his mother at any cost.

Integration into the local community was a joy. I was profoundly grateful to the kind and homely neighbours who accepted me as one of their own. They always referred to me as 'Mongan's Boy', never as Jimmy Dunne. This did not worry me unduly as I had no clear perception of who the Dunnes were, or where they actually came from. But one day I would find my brothers and sister.

Paddy Joe Molloy, from one of the neighbouring farms became a very special friend and together we hammered two discarded old bikes into one reasonably good one. Each night, after hastily splashing my face in the tin basin, I cycled with him to the local village square, where the lads played 'pitch and toss' and 'horseshoes'. Life was very good indeed for Mongan's boy.

Seven years on, I was still with the Mongans and had grown into a six-foot, dark haired, lean handsome man. Mrs. Mongan's words, not mine. I was full of confidence and a zest for living, far removed from the thin scared boy who left the industrial school years before. I owed a debt to gratitude to Mrs. Mongan who loved me and made a man of me. It was so fitting and natural that I should love her also.

## The Ireland We Remember

I sang all day as I worked, earning myself the nickname of 'Mongan's Lark'. I was the John McCormack of Caherdearg and it came as no surprise when I was asked to join the local church choir. Saturday nights were practice nights, and it was then that I met Sarah.

She was a real corker. Dainty, blonde and beautiful, with pearly white teeth and limpid green eyes. I was besotted from the first moment I saw her, and lost no time confiding in Mrs. Mongan, whose approval was of utmost importance to me. Our romance blossomed slowly and steadily over the next three years, with Mrs. Mongan's well-meant motherly advice cooling my ardour somewhat.

"Don't rush things, son," she said anxiously. "Give it time. Let it happen gradually and then both of ye will be absolutely sure."

It was so gradual that I went perilously close to losing Sarah. Young males didn't rush to the altar rails in those days. Many were in their mid-thirties, still going steady with their first love without a thought for marriage. Unconsciously, I had joined the Bachelor Club. But Sarah, at twenty three, was not into long term man-waiting and ultimately I had to reach a decision.

Sadly, the time came to leave Caherdearg and with it the realisation that I had no financial security whatsoever. Nothing to offer a young wife. Sarah and I decided to take the boat to England like all other couples who planned a life together. I dreaded leaving Mrs. Mongan, the only mother I had ever known, fearing she wouldn't cope with the work on her own. Her genuine grief tore at my heart when I told her Sarah and I were leaving.

"Yer doing the right thing," she whispered tearfully. "Ye'd never have anything of yer own, son, if ye remained with us. Sarah deserves the best ye can offer her."

I was replaced by a seventeen years old girl, who was not just pretty and fair-haired, but bright and bouncy with laughter lines all over her happy face. She was, I felt sure, a spirited young lady who would not be intimidated by Mr. Mongan's rough nature. It would be an enlightening experience for that man if he deliberately set about unnerving her.

I kept in touch with Mrs. Mongan, telling her of my life in London, my marriage to Sarah, and subsequently the birth of our baby boy whom I promised her would be introduced to Caherdearg before he could walk.

She showed remarkable survivability following the sudden demise of her husband some years later, and far from being crushed beneath this severe blow she was apparently given a new lease of life, harking back to her younger days when she was actively involved in the organising of local school concerts, the cleaning of the church, and above all else, the washing and starching of the altar linen. Only a selected few were chosen to perform this exalted task and Mrs. Mongan was one of them.

Sarah and I and our young son returned to Caherdearg every other year, always with the feeling that we were coming home. But our most memorable visit, at the specific command of Mrs. Mongan, proved to be both eventful and exciting. Unbeknown to us she had undertaken an exhaustive and sometimes futile search to find my brothers and sister, ably assisted by her parish priest and the superiors of that once detested industrial school in the west.

It was a joyous occasion, meeting my hitherto unknown family for the first time with Mrs. Mongan proudly performing the introductions. Emotionally overcome, I could only throw my arms around her and proclaim with deep sincerity,

"God Bless this wonderful woman, whom I am proud to call Mother in my heart."

# The Ireland We Remember

*The young, handsome Mongans boy*

CHAPTER 3

# Adopted Grandmother

MINUTES AFTER MY SIX-YEAR old brother, Danny, left for school on Monday morning, he dived back into our small farmhouse kitchen, agitated and distressed.

"Missus Moran is dead," he announced shakily, fear written all over his face.

"Who's that?" seven year old Jamie asked, clearly unimpressed.

"It's Grandmother, ye big eejit," Danny squeaked. "Grandmother is dead. Florrie told me to run home and tell."

A deadly silence followed. Florrie must have said 'Missus Moran', I thought, stuffing my lunch into my school bag. Danny would never say that.

"Not Grandmother," I said shrilly, my throat beginning to dry up. I was having difficultly swallowing.

"She wouldn't die," I told Danny courageously. "Bet it will all be a big fat lie when we come home from school."

## The Ireland We Remember

Suddenly he crumpled, and the tears which were threatening to blind him spilled down his thin little cheeks.

All three of us with our skinny little bodies, wide brown eyes, and brown curly hair, were shocked into silence - for once. The name 'Missus Moran' didn't mean anything to us children. But Grandmother did. She was Grandmother to each of us, all our short young lives. Her own granddaughter generally addressed her as Grandmother when she came for summer holidays. We just assumed that was her name, and believed we should call her Grandmother also.

Now Danny was sobbing that she was dead. She couldn't be. She was alive and well last night. She was such a tiny little woman, so frail, so old, to whom we ran with all our childish worries, in our small farming community. Her face was a leathery maze of cracks and lines, like a worn cowboy boot. But her bird-like blue eyes still held their youthful glint, and only on rare occasions did she resort to using her rimless glasses which she kept dangling from her neck on a faded brown shoe lace.

Finally, order was restored in our house as Mam tried, not very successfully, to calm us down, and eventually we were bundled off to school thirty minutes late. Concentration was virtually impossible. We could neither read nor write all day, and a waspish schoolmistress clouted us incessantly, as was the norm in those far away nineteen-thirties, accusing us of day-dreaming and wasting her time.

We fled home at 3.00pm. The hundred yards of boreen to our house ran along to the rear of Grandmother's, and most evenings at twilight, we sat on the low wall, outside her bedroom window, while we waited for her to open the back door and collect her pottie, which she had 'airing' all day, behind the old wooden barrel in the back yard. She would dig deep in a huge pocket underneath her apron, and produce one peppermint for each of us, telling us with a gummy smile,

"Now, run aways home to yer mother, d'ye hear me?"

We knew her every move. She usually went straight to her bedroom while we sat outside and watched her undress, consumed with curiosity as to how many layers of clothing would be peeled off, before she finally climbed into bed. We had seen it all so many times before, yet it never failed to intrigue. First, she removed her black shawl from her shoulders and placed it carefully over the back of the cane chair in the corner. Then she untied her black satin apron, folding it neatly beside the shawl. Next to her shawl were her black blouse and black skirt, followed by a heavy red petticoat. A white bodice and underskirt were exchanged for a long flannelette nightshirt, buttoned up tightly to her neck. As she stood for a moment in front of the Sacred Heart picture, she let her long white hair fall loosely on her shoulders. Picking up her huge rosary beads from the little table with the white cloth, she turned to the window, fully aware that we were still sitting there, even if she couldn't see us in the gathering dusk, to say with mock severity,

"If ye don't go home, I'll wallop yer backsides!"

We giggled. We knew she wouldn't.

We looked at the window now, on our way home from school, with it's blind drawn. There was an air of unreality about the place. We could feel something was very wrong. Nervousness overcame us, and we hurriedly ran the short distance to our home. That evening we pestered Mam to allow us to look in at Grandmother, secretly hoping to find she was just sleeping. She was propped up slightly, against snowy white pillows, trimmed with black lace, with the familiar rosary beads entwined in her hands. Lighted candles, spluttering in brass candlesticks stood on her little bedside table, casting eerie shadows around the small room. We stood by her bed in bewildered silence, gripping each other's hands tightly. Suddenly Jamie, who could never remain silent for long, hissed loudly,

"That's not Grandmother. That's a man!"

Danny and I agreed that 'he' didn't look in the least like Grandmother. I detested that awful brown thing she was wearing. Years later I learned it was called a 'habit'. It certainly did nothing for her colour. Danny pinched me hard and whispered,

"She's watching us Peg. I can see her."

One eye was not quite closed and it seemed to stare in our direction. As the breeze from the open window caused the candles to flicker, the light moved in Grandmother's eye, giving the impression, in our highly nervous state, that she was actually looking at us. Terror gripped us, and we scuttled from the room like scared rabbits, almost knocking each other in our efforts to make a hasty exit.

Grandmother's daughter-in-law, Florrie, took us into the kitchen for biscuits, calmly assuring us that everything was all right. Grandmother was gone to God, she told us, and would be looking down at us at all times, so we had better be good. We stood close together, deliberately refraining from looking towards the room again, while we hastily munched Florrie's biscuits. Our fear must have been obvious to all. Old John Moore, sitting in the armchair by the kitchen fire, smoking his clay pipe, said quietly, without looking up,

"Run them kids home Florrie. They're too young."

Turning to me he said, "Go on Pegeen. You're the oldest. Bring them lads home."

I was, in fact, eight years old but Jamie and Danny possessed more intellect than I ever did, Mom always said. We were such imaginative children. Nothing was impossible in our make-believe world.

Memories of her remained with us constantly after she passed away. We could recall with total clarity her way of leaning forward with both bony hands on her walking cane, as she sat on her stone seat on the hill close by her home. Her seat was a huge rock jutting out from the wall, well polished from years of constant use and known to all as 'Grandmother's seat'.

Slowly and laboriously, she shuffled her way to her seat each summer day, to look down and watch the green fields turn to gold, in readiness for a bumper harvest. How we loved the strong odour of Sloan's Liniment that emanated from her clothes. We had counted all the deep craggy lines in her face, and marvelled that she could keep her thinning white hair fastened so securely in a 'bun' with huge hair pins and combs. Jamie, always the cheeky one, habitually sneaked up behind her back, while she surveyed the village from on high, to withdraw the pins, and watch fascinated, as her silvery hair cascaded to her shoulders.

"Put them back," she would order, lifting her cane as if to hit him.

She never did, of course. We knew how kind she was. We always knew she loved us, and Danny and I climbed onto her knee, while Jamie prodded and poked, to get the pins, and the hair, back into place. We listened in awe when she told us that soon, very soon, she would receive a present from the President, for reaching the ripe old age of one hundred years. Afterwards, we could never remember the word 'President', and told our young friends at school that the King was coming with Grandmother's present.

Contrary to instructions from our burly sheep-farming father, we continued to sit huddled together each evening on the low wall outside her bedroom window, hoping... for what, we didn't really know. We missed her unbearably. Her passing had a profound effect on us. We just sat there, and wished her back.

Perhaps if we called her, she might hear us, I suggested, one chilly evening. Instantly, Danny was on his feet, circling his mouth with his hands, to call long and loud into the westerly wind, "Grandmother! Grandmother!"

She didn't answer. Only his echo returned faintly, 'Grandmo-ther, -other, -other!'

Perhaps she got deaf since she left, Jamie offered, helpfully, oblivious of the fact that Grandmother was always very deaf indeed.

"We'll try again. All together this time," Danny said, hope springing eternal once more.

Our lungs would never be the same again. Throats were scratchy and hope fading, when Jamie suddenly yelled excitedly,

"There she is. Over there! She's coming!"

"We're here Grandmother," Danny called out to the spot where Jamie was pointing to.

"She's like the man in the moon," I shouted, as excitement intensified, although I couldn't see her too clearly, with racing clouds obscuring my vision, just as I thought she was coming towards us.

But she was there. We knew she was. With her pottie partly hidden beneath her shiny black apron. Grandmother was there. She hadn't forgotten us. We pranced around delighted, waving and shouting,

"We see you Grandmother!" And then her voice floated down to us on the breeze,

"If ye don't go home, I'll wallop yer backsides."

This time we DID go home, but not before we had exhausted ourselves completely. Mam ruffled our dark curly heads, and smiled softly to herself, as we blurted out our sensational story, while she tucked us into our warm feather beds.

Despite our most valiant efforts to stay awake, our eyelids closed firmly, while we happily listed all the nice things we had to tell Grandmother, when she would appear from behind the clouds tomorrow evening.

# Anne Morrin

*Grandmother*

CHAPTER 4

# The Black Melodeon

It was the proudest moment of my nine-year old life, the moment when James Devaney asked me, Kathleen O' Shea, to pick up his daily paper at the local post office after school. He trusted me. He actually entrusted me with his all-important newspaper. I swelled with pride. That I should be singled out from all the other village children to perform this noble task, as we picked blackberries on the roadside on our way home from school. I looked from one to the other of my companions, fully expecting to see their faces green with envy. Instead, their mouths and hands were amply smudged with the purple-black juice from the blackberries, and they hadn't even noticed James as he pushed his bicycle against the steep hill.

"I'm too busy to collect the paper myself," he told me, as he led me away from the others to speak privately, "but I know yerself will bring it to me without tearin' it."

Oh, I would. He could rest assured I would. That paper would be treated like my schoolbooks – with the greatest of care. The Devaneys never called me by my name. They just said, "Is that yerself?" I had no answer to that. I smiled instead.

It puzzled me to hear James say he was too busy to collect his paper. He never exerted himself. Many hours of his day were spent snoozing in the armchair by the fire. I knew, because I went there frequently for apples at harvest time. There was a huge orchard to the front of their thatched house. It was the proud possessor of thirty-six apple trees. I counted them every week.

They produced cooking and eating apples of every description. It was a magical moment each time I stood in that orchard, gazing at all the glorious reds and greens like beautiful coloured balloons, and finding it well nigh impossible to choose.

The Devaneys lived across the fields from our house. They were known as 'well-off' farmers as they owned more land and cattle and sheep than the other village farmers. People said they had money and knew how to 'salt it away'. To get to Devaney's house I had to climb over the high wall which divided our farms, sending sheep scurrying in all directions when I dropped down on the other side.

James had my promise to deliver his paper immediately after school but my mother had other plans, insisting that I eat dinner first. That way she could scan the paper herself and relay the news to my father who refused outright to read that particular paper, as its politics differed from the one he purchased himself on fair days once a month. He never commented on any news items my mother read out to him except to say sourly,

"What does that crowd know anyway?"

My mother would then fold the paper carefully, smoothing out the edges lest James should suspect her of reading it. I would scamper off happily through the fields secure in the knowledge that I would get the princely sum of ONE penny

## The Ireland We Remember

on Friday evenings for a week's delivery well done. I never knew if he got a paper on Saturdays. He never said.

James Devaney was a 'sober-sides' whilst his brother Michael was a humorist forever telling little jokes that I, in my innocence, failed to recognize as funny. Just the same, I laughed to please him. He looked expectantly, like a friendly dog awaiting a pat on the head, and whilst I didn't understand his jocularity, I sensed his pleasure at my apparent appreciation of his witticisms.

Their sister Bridget who was in her late sixties, as they were, was a small round bundle, a mere four-foot-nine inches high, with a pale wrinkled face and shoulder-length wavy grey hair, which she plaited at the back and tied with a piece of gingham left over from making an apron. Like most children in our village, I was slightly apprehensive at our first meeting but that was at the tender age of six. In the intervening years, I gradually came to realize that she was kind and generous and extremely fond of children.

Bridget had seventy free-range hens. Their eggs were washed with my help and put into two baskets in readiness for the 'travelling shop', with which she dealt for all her household needs. The price of a score of eggs varied from week to week, and as Bridget had several score to sell, the 'egg money' very often exceeded the price of her groceries, in which case she had 'change' to collect – much to the chagrin of the grocer. He would exert himself trying to cajole her into buying something else – anything was preferable to parting with that change. But Bridget was a wily old bird. She would stuff her money into her apron pocket with a sassiness that silenced the grocer instantly. On the rare occasions that I didn't break an egg during washing she treated me to a huge round currant biscuit when she did her shopping. She fed her brothers well with good wholesome food, chiefly bacon, cabbage and potatoes. In my young mind they resembled great big fat snails moving ever so slowly, their bloated red faces partly hidden beneath broad rimmed hats, which they pulled down to their ears to safeguard them from 'risin' on windy days.

I didn't have to ask for the paper. The local postmaster had been previously notified and the paper with 'James Devaney' scrawled across the front page was left on the windowsill awaiting my arrival after school. The postmaster was a garrulous man. He usually enquired about my parents, looking at me over the top of his broken glasses, rattling off anything that entered his head. Most evenings he told me,

"Yer far too thin. Ye don't take after yer mother's people. They had plenty of 'mate' on their bones. Yer goin' to be lanky and fair like yer oul' fella."

He was constantly complaining about the cold even on warm summer days, and always warmed his hands on the globe of the hanging paraffin lamp, which he kept lighted all day long. The lamp was slung low on long chains to provide him with warmth while he stood behind the dark wooden counter, which also served as a grocery counter. He placed a sheet of heavy brown paper next to his hairy chest inside his woollen vest to retain the heat. Never had I seen such a thin cold man, with his long sunken jaws and bony arthritic hands.

Occasionally James Devaney instructed me to ask for twenty Players and to 'put them on the bill'. A jotter was produced from beneath the counter and after much pen suckin' the cigarettes were duly charged. The postmaster kept a stock of old writing pens with wooden holders and brass coloured nibs in an old red jug on the shelf. He selected one, and then another, when the first failed to write. The scratching and scraping made my teeth water. He would never discard the worn out nibs, fervently hoping to get another 'go' if he gave them 'a rest'.

I actually looked forward to collecting that paper for James. The grocery end of the post office always smelled of barm-brack and caraway seeds and if the man himself was in a good mood, I just might get one Bullseye.

James permitted himself one cigarette per day. On Sodality Saturdays after confessions, he 'did' the books for that worthy organization, 'The Pioneer Total Abstinence Association', of which he was treasurer. He held his cigarette in his hand with his little finger stretched out in much the same way as nice old ladies held their dainty china teacups with their ridiculously small handles.

He was held in high esteem in the parish. People went to him on Saturdays to consult him about their old age pensions, should their long awaited two and six pence fail to materialize on reaching seventy years of age.

The Devaneys had a profound interest in my schoolteacher whom they told me was 'reported to be a bit cross'. Eager to show off, I always jumped up, delighted to have such an assiduous audience and demonstrated my teacher's method of caning us, leaving our hands lumpy and sore. I left nothing out. The men would look at each other silently, while Bridget sat on the turf box by the fire pleating her toothless mouth between her thumb and forefinger. I saw no reason for their loud guffaws of laughter when I told them solemnly that my father said,

"That woman is a bloody monster," and my mother's sharp rebuke,

"Don't say that in front of you-know-who. She'll only carry it."

In my far off salad years, I was very naïve and had no idea then that Teacher was in fact their sister, ten years younger than Bridget.

Having the Stations was a once in seven years event in the nineteen-thirties. The priest came in the early morning to say Mass. It was a special day with the entire village congregating to hear the Mass and pay their dues. Months of preparation went into this special occasion. All the accumulated rubbish in the house had to be thrown out, much of it to be returned gradually once the great day was over, and the entire house painted and scrubbed.

Now it was Devaneys turn. I helped Bridget to carry heaps of things up to the loft in the barn. That was when I discovered the black melodeon tucked away on the bottom shelf of the glass-case in the parlour. I was useless to Bridget from that moment. The melodeon became my constant companion. I practiced on it at every opportune moment. The exquisite joy of holding a musical instrument in my hands! Years later, during the Pope's visit to Ireland when all the churches reverberated to the sound of *'He's got the whole world in his hands'*, I thought again of the black melodeon and how I had felt that I too had the whole world in my hands on that wonderful, memorable day when I found it.

Teacher always said I had an ear for music. Apparently I had. Within two weeks I could pick out the notes of a tune I had heard on my uncle's gramophone many, many times, impressed no doubt by its rather amusing title *'If I got Maggie in the Wood'*.

Bridget's rubbish was forgotten although I knew she was getting on with the job from the ever-increasing mountain in the corner of the loft. She supplied me with a wooden box for my precious melodeon until the stations were over, when it would once more be returned to its rightful place in the parlour.

"Don't drag it so much," Bridget chided me gently one day. "You'll break it in two."

It had belonged to their grandmother, she told me, and was one of their dearest possessions. How honoured I felt when she added, "We wouldn't let anyone touch it, only yerself." James insisted that I keep to the loft when I boldly took it into the kitchen one evening to exhibit my skills. The noise was hurting his ears, he told me. I was happy to oblige. No one would disturb me there. Oul' Rover, their faithful black dog, who was as big and as fat as his owners, was my only audience. He sat on the steps leading up to the loft, watching me with such beseeching eyes, while he waited for the crusts he knew I had stuck inside my jumper. His piercing wails would rent the calm evening air when I hit the high notes, and his paw would come up to flick his ear almost as if it hurt.

"He's pretending he's James," I thought and bashed on regardless.

Disaster struck on the evening when I got too cheeky and decided to have 'one go' on the melodeon BEFORE I delivered the paper to the ever-patient James. There were no crusts for Rover and he consoled himself with ripping the pages to shreds while I had eyes for nothing but my little black box.

Tears of humiliation and shame spilled down my thin pale cheeks as I presented James with the tattered remains of his paper. He patted my head with his big fat hand, telling me not to cry. Michael came to my rescue by saying jokingly,

"I suppose Rover likes to chew on the daily news like ourselves."

Returning to the loft later on with Rover I scolded him furiously.

"Never, ever again," I shouted, close to tears once more. "Never will I leave the paper near you again, and never, ever will you get another crust."

Rover looked so dejected and mournful that my anger evaporated rapidly. Five minutes later all was forgiven and I was back in Bridget's kitchen in search of a crust.

The day came when they purchased a wireless – the first of its kind in our area, and the village men would gather in each night to hear the ten-fifteen news. Regretfully, James cancelled his daily paper at the post office and I was made redundant. To make certain that I would remain close to my music I promised them that I would come and see them every evening,

"Even when I'm grown up and married," I vowed, with all the sincerity of a nine year old.

On my last delivery evening, James pointed to the turf box on which lay a bulky parcel tied with twine.

"We'd like ye to have that," he told me, his face a bit redder than usual.

Consumed with curiosity, I hastily undid the twine and there wrapped up in layers of old newspapers was………. you've guessed it……….. the black melodeon! I looked uncertainly from one to the other. They couldn't be parting with their treasured heirloom, I thought. Astonishment and then sheer joy abounded in my heart as I looked at their faces and knew I wasn't mistaken.

"Go on, take it. It's for yerself," Michael urged me. "Take good care of it now."

Then, with his usual jocularity, he smiled and said, "Maybe some day ye'll catch up with '*Maggie in the Wood*'."

## The Ireland We Remember

*Collecting the paper after school*

CHAPTER 5

# The Cockney Farmer

"Shove on these boots and run out for the cows," Uncle Tom said, pushing the wellingtons in my direction, and giving me a firm push towards the kitchen door.

"The earlier the better, before the flies get busy in this hot weather," he offered by way of apology for dragging me out of bed at six in the morning.

"Flippin' 'ell," I muttered savagely under my breath. Indeed, I could have said it aloud for all the difference it made. Uncle couldn't 'make out' my cockney accent. Whenever I spoke I was met with a blank stare and a frustrated,

"Hah? What's that yer sayin'?"

While I pulled on the four-sizes-too-large-wellingtons I wished my Irish mom was around so that I could tell her what I thought of her precious birthplace and her rugged farmer brother. It was her idea to send me back 'home' every year as a youngster to gain practical experience on the family farm. I was a sausages-and-water boy in those days, and a

finicky eater such as I was had to 'take it or leave it' many times. Uncle relished his bacon and cabbage. He boiled half a pig's head once and the glassy eye seemed to stare accusingly in my direction as we sat down to dinner. Uncle commenced carving and asked me,
"Would'ja like a bit o' the shnout?"
I fled from the table and threw up.

Getting a hair-cut was something of an endurance test. That man didn't just cut my hair. He sheared me and nicked me so badly in the process that the top of my head resembled a battle field without the bodies. Uncle was the Sweeney Todd of my youth.

It was the world that changed it all eventually. The gradual intrusion of other things in my life ..... new friends, new interests, and the annual trips were put on hold until I was seventeen, when my parents persuaded me to return - no doubt to keep me from wandering the streets through the long summer vacation.

"The farm is the ideal place for the holidays, Tommy," my mother insisted.

"Ye'll be a fountain of knowledge when you return in September."

I couldn't agree less as I walked through the dew-drenched grass to bring in the cows for the early morning milking.

"Come on, come on," Uncle urged as I prepared to make a hasty exit from the cow-shed once the cows were in.

"Get some wather and wash down that lot," he said, gesturing towards the bucket near the door.

I washed their udders with indifference, but the cows, who were familiar with Uncle's movements and mutterings, treated me with contemptible scepticism and reacted to my slapdash methods in the only way they knew - by raising their tails and performing in no uncertain manner, making my empty stomach churn sickeningly, while Uncle walked up and down through it all clearly unconcerned. Where, oh where were those immaculate 'Kerry Gold workers' we had become so familiar with when we got our first telly, I wondered, as I got a lash of a stinking greeny tail across my unsuspecting face. The stench remained in my nostrils for hours.

Uncle switched on a transistor radio and treated the cows to some music.

"They love it," he said, noting my incredulous stare and jiving a little to the strains of *'Go Johnny, go, go, go'* with laughter in his eyes.

Flippin' nut case, I reckoned. But a 'noice' one, I amended hastily. After all, I was going to live with him for eight weeks.

"Scratch their rumps while they're milkin'," Uncle advised one morning when my presence was obviously unsettling his animals.

"They won't let down the milk if they notice yeh strange," he explained patiently.

"Now don't let them know yer nervous," he cautioned, as I took up position between two of them and commenced scratching as he himself was doing.

To my everlasting surprise they responded instantly. This was a major breakthrough for me. Success on that never-to-be-forgotten morning was like heady wine. I felt I had really achieved something. Uncle grinned with satisfaction.

"See what I mean?" he said knowingly. Unfortunately for me in my crass ignorance, I assumed that rump-scratching extended to the big red Hereford bull in the far field. Only when he lunged at me in fury with nostrils flaring and I was forced to run for my life, did I realise the enormity of my foolishness. It didn't help to see Uncle panting and red-faced running to my rescue with the pitch-fork in his hand. I expected an earful.

"Yer an awful eejit," he gasped, throwing himself on the ground while I sprinted to safety on his side of the fence.

"Wouldn't yeh think the look of him would've warned yeh he's dangerous," he panted irritably. It didn't. I was no more of an authority on animal moods than Uncle was on climbing Mount Everest.

"When yeh see a twelve-hundhurt weight bull lumberin' around the field it's hard to believe he can run faster than ye," Uncle said, and added grimly, "But don't ever put it to the test if ye want to see *Elephant and Camels* again."

"Put it down to experience," he advised, "and never, ever forget it."

Deciding to overlook my stupidity, he hit me playfully across the shoulders with one of his bone-rattling slaps and said,

"D'ye know what, Cockney, we'll make a farmer o' yeh yet."

When the fear of being gored by the bull receded, Uncle regained his composure sufficiently to satisfy my curiosity, with graphic details of the important role that highly temperamental animal played in the expansion of his herd each year.

"Come back in the spring," he suggested, "an' ye'll see the fruits of his labours for yerself." I suddenly realised how totally inadequate my farming knowledge was, despite my Irish background, and from there on I developed a healthy respect for the fickleness of these creatures especially in the male domain. Incredible as it may seem, I actually acquired a 'taste' for farming during that long summer. Tiring certainly, but most rewarding. I derived immense pleasure from aping Uncle by closing one eye and pulling the peak of my borrowed cap well down over the other eye, before glancing shrewdly and sharply at each cow as they ambled out after milking.

"Don't let that 'wan' go. She needs a dose," Uncle shouted occasionally when he suspected one of his herd was unusually listless, and the day that I also learned to 'spot a wrong wan' was a great day indeed. Such clever detection all on my own made me swell with pride and had Uncle laughing uncontrollably.

"Didn't I tell yeh we'd make a farmer o' yeh, Cockney," he croaked, spluttering and guffawing at the same time.

"Cor Blimey! Me 'mites' won't ruddy believe any of this," I thought excitedly. Most of them had no idea of what cows looked like apart from television's squeaky clean version... The 'K.G.W's as we knew them.

I returned to Ireland in the spring-time as Uncle suggested, anxious to get back to the farm. It was another world, far removed from the constant rush and the overcrowded pavements of London. I arrived in time to witness the births of several red Hereford calves. Uncle and I had little sleep, often waiting for hours during a prolonged or difficult delivery, but the instant a healthy youngster slithered to the ground I knew a satisfaction and pride incomparable with anything I had ever experienced in my life.

"There's a few 'hundhurt' quids worth there," Uncle declared with much lip-smacking, admiring the pen of frisky new-born calves, and I could only nod my head in silence at the wonder of it all.

"Would'ja ever think of coming over for good?" he asked casually, shooting a spit between his teeth that reached halfway across the calf-pen.

"I'm not exactly 'skint'," he added, reaching for a straw to chew on.

"We'd make a great team with yeh at the helm."

Helm or stern, it was irrelevant, I knew what I wanted.

"Give me one year to finish college, then I'm back," I promised.

## The Ireland We Remember

"Welcome aboard, Cockney," he smiled with a bone-crushing squeeze of my hand.

*Springtime on the farm*

CHAPTER 6

# Cockney's Return

I PROMISED UNCLE I'D come back as soon as I finished college. Back to Ireland to the cows and the calves and the farm smells that churned my insides as a young lad.
I was brought up on a diet of exhaust-pipe and factory fumes, living around Elephant and Castle in London, but summer holidays in Ireland with Uncle and his cows introduced me to equally unpleasant odours which I managed to overcome quite well with time. The day I could trudge through the muck like Uncle and ignore the stench, was the day I became a man, he reckoned.
We were going to make a great team, Uncle and I. He had big plans for modernising his stock-breeding methods, but had difficulty for some time accepting the fact that new procedures could not be implemented in the old way. Therefore, I was immensely relieved to know the big red bull in the far field was sold before my arrival. I hadn't forgotten my brief encounter with that savage two years earlier. I was so

naive then, never realizing that a farm could be so fraught with danger.

The bull had outlived his usefulness, apparently, and was replaced by the 'A.I. Man', whom Uncle disapproved of, but had little choice in the matter if he wanted this thing called progress.

"What's he got in that straw he carries around between his teeth?" I asked in my ignorance, the first time I saw the A.I. man in action.

"A young Friesen calf," Uncle explained importantly, adding,

"God, yer fierce thick over there in Elephant and fotch'a-ma-call-it. Ye know nothin'," forgetting that he himself refused to know anything about A.I. until recently.

He was a great believer in 'Oul' Mother Nature' and while he knew in his heart that 'Red Harry', as he called the bull, would have to go, he was just a little bit sceptical of artificial insemination, and 'them young gits' breezin' into the yard with the whole works in the boot o' the car'.

No one was more surprised than he was when the cows produced their first crop of healthy Friesen calves.

"It can't be right, all the same", he persisted doggedly. Change did not come easily to Uncle, or indeed any of the farmers of his time, and 'Red Harry's' redundancy pricked his conscience more than he cared to admit. We were in this together now, I reminded him. I had left London behind, and the opportunity to study for electrical engineering was put on hold indefinitely. Cockney I might be, and I was certainly no expert, but if common sense prevailed, I felt I could be relied upon not to make rash decisions

We rose at 6 a.m. daily. Uncle was a great one for the 'early bird' bit. London was an early riser also, something I utterly detested throughout my school years. But all that changed in after-days in Ireland. It became one of the joys of my life to go out at dawn and watch the sun creep high into a cloudless sky. To watch the sleeping village come to life slowly, as one by one the chimneys puffed out the first plumes of blue smoke, and to greet the cheery neighbour who yelled 'How 'ya Cock-e-ney' on his way to milk the cow for his ageing mother.

At such times Uncle hovered around anxiously, mistaking my contentment for loneliness.

"Yeh wouldn't be thinkin' o' goin' back to them *Elephants and Camels* would 'yeh?" he asked as if he dreaded my reply.

Nothing, I assured him, would induce me to return to London. I was here to stay.

The cows waddled into the milking-parlour each morning when Sailor, the collie dog, rounded them up.

"Trying to nick me bleedin' job, is he?" I quipped, remembering all the times I walked through the dew-drenched grass as a youngster, to bring them in, while the dog lay at the back-door waiting for the rind from Uncle's four thick rashers, and generous man that he was, he was not averse to sharing a little of MY waiting breakfast if the dog looked longingly at the pan.

Blimey! Uncle had finally come to realise that 'having a dog and barking yourself' was just not practical. Another example of the winds of change, perhaps.

Growing up as I did on a busy London road with its vast volumes of traffic continually on the move, I found the silence eerie as I lay awake at night listening to the occasional unfamiliar country sounds. Now and then that silence was shattered by a tom-cat trying to seduce his mate directly beneath my window. The piercing screeches sent me diving beneath the blankets to block out the sound. Equally shrill were the strident calls of his lady-friend while she played 'hard to get' and scurried over the garden wall, only to return seconds later and tantalize him all over again.

## The Ireland We Remember

I asked Uncle if I could borrow the cow's radio at night, hoping to get some sleep. He consented grudgingly... but "yeh betther have that back in the shed in the mornin' or there'll be no milk," he warned. Just like the old days. Music while you milk. At least with the radio going full blast I would not have to endure the nerve-racking guttural sounds coming from his room when he snored loudly after a few pints on Saturday nights. The spooky silence, despite giving me the creeps, was much easier on the ear.

Uncle purchased an ancient tractor and mini-trailer to transport the milk to the creamery when I was seventeen. Slightly envious of his ability to manoeuvre his machinery so adeptly with all the milk-churns on board, I foolishly suggested that I be allowed to exhibit my imaginary driving skills through the village.

"D'yeh want to kill the pair 'oos?" he roared, his face flushed with anger.

He shook his head in disbelief at such audacity, bellowing,

"John Bull is sthill rearin' them, it seems."

He laughed heartily at the memory three years later when I produced my first full driving-licence and asked with feigned modesty,

"Can I have a go now, UNK?"

That old tractor was behaving erratically at the end of my first year on the farm. Like 'Red Harry' it had outlived its usefulness and had to be replaced with something better. Uncle swore like a trooper at first, refusing to admit that it was no longer road-worthy, but eventually he capitulated as I hoped he would. We prepared for spring with much more reliable equipment, albeit second-hand, which we reckoned would see us safely through the next few years.

We were in urgent need of transport for ourselves also. I shared a rickety old bike with Uncle.....which posed a problem when both of us wanted it at the same time. We solved

43

our dilemma by purchasing a second-hand bike for me. Not surprisingly, Uncle refused to relinquish his own antiquated model. Surely a new bike for each of us wouldn't break the bank, I thought irritably. We had a substantial cheque from the creamery each month which he predicted we'd need 'out there'. Was he just a tight-fisted oul' codger? I couldn't be sure. I was prepared to humour him until all the calves were sold, and our bank account indicated that penny-pinching was no longer necessary, and certainly not acceptable. We made considerable progress in that year with which Uncle was pleasantly surprised and happy. But soon he wanted more.

"We'll have to try an' getcha a woman next year," he declared, poker-faced.

"She'd be handy around the place."

Flippin' 'ell, 'im an' 'ees bleedin' match-making! Would I be expected to share her also? A million thoughts chased furiously through my seething brain. He could keep his stupid Irish crap. I was barely out of college, for chris'sake. I'd jolly well scupper his plans.......

"Find a second-hand one for yourself," I scoffed rudely, hoping to annoy him. Instead he guffawed loudly, tears of laughter streaming unheeded down his grimy face.

"God, ye'd believe anythin'," he croaked at last when he recovered his breath.

"Yer an awful eejit, Cockney.......but a fierce nice wan all the same," he amended when he could control his laughter.

We worked hard throughout the winter, feeding the cows indoors. Uncle mucked out daily with his barrow, sweat dripping untended from the top of his nose.

"Its hellish hard work, dhrawin' into them an' dhrawn' out from them," he complained wearily.

I suggested hesitantly that a minimal investment from the calf-sales would scale down that particular work-load considerably, and surprisingly, he agreed readily. Very soon spring was establishing itself after a dreary winter. That wondrous time of new life and new hope on the farm. I was proud and happy to be part of it.

London and its skyscrapers seemed a million miles away......

*Our first introduction to machinery*

# CHAPTER 7

# Cockney's Mom

"WHAT THE HECK IS bringin' 'er over here this time o' the year. Wouldn't yeh think she'd wait'll summer?" Uncle grumbled, throwing down the letter impatiently. The long-awaited news had arrived at last from my Mom. She was coming from London to visit us for St. Patrick's Day. It seemed to take forever before she finally decided to come. I had almost despaired of seeing the postman stopping at our gate ever again.

"I wouldn't mind HER," Uncle was fond of saying, "sure, that woman doesn't know whether she's comin' or goin' half the times. She'll turn up when yeh least expect 'er."

Mom was not a great correspondent at the best of times. "Yeh wouldn't know anyone over there, so there's no point in writin' about them," she'd try to explain to Uncle, and he'd hit back with, "for all yeh write, ye'd fit it on the back oo' stamp."

She had an early morning job, which together with housekeeping and looking after my brothers and dad, kept her continually on her toes. A mountain of domestic chores awaited her attention prior to her departure. It was great news. I could hardly wait for the day. Practically three years ago I decided to leave London behind and move to Mom's birthplace, where I became a 'Cockney farmer'.

"The first of yer kind in Ireland," Uncle teased.

I never regretted my decision. Ireland was where I wanted to be, but now that Mom's visit was about to become a reality, I had a sudden overwhelming longing to see her again and catch up on the family news she so rarely wrote about. Uncle seemed unable to share my enthusiasm.

"She'll have ever'thin' flung out there the minute she comes," he predicted irritably, pointing to the backdoor with nicotine-stained fingers. "But I'll tell yeh somethin'," he assured me, "I'll have ever'thin' back in, just as fast as she flings them out. I know 'er oul' capers. Spring-clanin' my foot. She cannot sit down for a second."

We didn't hear from her again. She began her long journey from Euston station to Holyhead, in time to catch the boat to Dun Laoghaire. From there she got a train to the city, and yet another train from there to Galway, arriving in time for west-bound travellers to board the Clifden/Cong bus for home. I could scarcely contain myself when it finally pulled over to where I stood waiting in the rain. Every other passenger seemed to squeeze out the door ahead of Mom, but eventually she appeared, dragging a large clumsy suitcase behind her. Three years faded into oblivion in seconds. She was exactly as I remembered her, and when she giggled and said,

"Well, YOU haven't changed much," I could truthfully say, "Neither have you, Mom."

"What have you got in the case, apart from clothes?" I asked curiously, while I struggled to lift it on to the carrier of my bike.

"Just an 'oul blanket an' a hot-water bottle," she replied, as if it was customary to haul such things on holidays. "Actually," she confided hesitantly, noting my puckered brow, "there is no spare blanket for that rickety oul' bed in the back room."

"That reminds me," she added briskly, "that bed could be damp and in need of drying out before I rest my weary bones on it."

Weary was not a word one could associate with my mother. She was so full of boundless energy that you could feel exhausted just watching her skim through her chores. Suddenly, I felt an enormous sense of guilt. Why had it never occurred to me to check that flippin' bed? Perhaps that was Mom's fault as much as mine. A legacy from the days of 'Mom'll fix it', when she did every little thing for her family and never expected us to do anything for her in return. It was quite obvious that she took it all in her stride. She was a regular visitor to the old homestead with her children down through the years, and not one to be fazed by dampness or other tiresome problems that confronted her frequently. We never noticed such things as children. Our interest lay in chasing the hens and chickens in the back garden from the moment we arrived. Uncle gave us a telling-off for that many times, complaining that the hens 'were throwin'' soft eggs from them' as a result of our harassment.

After tea Mom took down the bedclothes and spread them over the backs of the chairs in front of the open fire. The kitchen became steam-filled as the clothes dried out, and the smell of dampness wound its way to the smoky rafters. The mattress required considerable heat-treatment also, and Mom's bones must have been very weary indeed when she finally climbed into a reasonably warm bed at midnight.

Next morning, Uncle tip-toed from his bedroom, hugging his chamber pot tightly beneath his heavy frieze overcoat.

"She's not goin' to get 'er hands on it, 'an that's for sure," he muttered, darting out the back door, with baleful looks at Mom's bedroom as he fled.

"For chris'sake, Unk, what would she want that for?" I enquired testily, suspecting over-reaction as usual.

"She'd have friggin' geraniums planted in it before nightfall," he spluttered, and disappeared into the cowshed.

He need not have worried. Mom went off to the well for a bucket of spring water. Good clear drinking water didn't come out of taps, she reckoned, and remembering how vivacious she always was, I felt certain she wouldn't pass up an opportunity to stop and chat with the neighbours on her way. It was as if she never left the village. She loved 'home', tramping through the fields regardless of weather conditions and enjoying the free and easy ways of yester-year.

I could not resist the temptation to share Uncle's secret dilemma with her. Neither could she resist having a go at him and with devilment in her eye she said, ever so innocently,

"Th'oul fella always kep' an oul' chamber-pot under the bed years ago, Tom. If I searched around outside, maybe I'd find it?"

"For wha?" he asked suspiciously.

"Well...." she replied, still looking angelic, "I was thinkin' it would look nice in the kitchen window with a bundle o' shamrock for St Patrick's Day."

That got his dander up. The wrathful look in my direction clearly said,

"Wha' did I tell yeh?" He decided to cut her down to size immediately, reminding her that such 'veshels' were obsolete for decades.

"It just goes to prove how backward ye are, over there in *Elephant and Camels*," he burst out arrogantly. "No one around here knows anythin' about them yokes. They were outta t'Ark. I'd be ashamed if anawan' heard yeh spoutin' that bull."

There! That ought to 'soften 'er cough for 'er', he thought, while his shrewd brain warned him there was no safe hiding place from his inquisitive sister. His face looked so red and angry, I could no longer contain my laughter, and he rounded on me with,

"Friggin' Cockney, humbuggin' me are yeh? Yer fierce smart now when yeh have yer mother backin' yeh up." But the relief in his voice was unmistakable as he strode out the door.

Two days into Mom's visit I could almost sympathise with Uncle. He didn't take kindly to this 'spring-clanin' he predicted so accurately from long experience. There was a hollow sound in the kitchen. The cat and dog felt eviction was imminent and fought desperately to retain possession of the tattered old settle-bed in the corner. Uncle wore a pained expression on his face and practically lived in the cowshed, conveniently forgetting the place was getting a face-lift without so much as him having to lift a finger.

"Mom gone to Mass?" I asked casually when she didn't appear for breakfast on St Patrick's morning.

"'Deed she's not," Uncle mumbled through his rashers, "she's out in the fields rootin' for shamrock. We'll hav'ta wear a shafe o'greenery on our jackets today.... the cows o' the parish'll be after us," he added, laughing heartily at his own joke.

All too soon Mom was preparing to leave us. "Come back with me, son," she pleaded. "Its lovely here but yeh work too hard. Ye'll find a good job in London. After all, yer hardly goin' to spend the rest o' yer life muckin' out cowsheds are yeh? Ye'll never get rich at the farmin'," she declared.

"I don't particularly want to," I laughed, hugging her gratefully for her concern.

"How could I survive in London without my cows and calves?" I teased.

## The Ireland We Remember

"Yeh always had a bit o' the Paddy in yeh," she smiled, slapping me playfully.

"I'm the happiest Cockney in Ireland," I assured her, and meant every word.

*Mom loved hay-making*

CHAPTER 8

# Cockney Goes For Gold

"Ye'r only gettin' married, Cockney, not becomin' President elect," Uncle grumbled irritably, unable to tolerate the commotion all around him.

"The cheek o'yeh anaway," Mom shouted from the backdoor where she was busy polishing shoes. "Miserable oul' git," she added impishly, well aware that her brother detested 'havin' everthin' in the house turned upside down by that busy-body every time she came home from England'.

Mom was over for my big day. So was Dad and my brother Sean, although she did not entirely approve of dragging them all the way to Mayo for a few days. Absolute waste of good money, she reckoned, and while she shared a certain empathy with Cathy for insisting on a traditional Irish wedding, she still maintained, privately of course, that St. George's Cathedral, so close to Elephant and Castle, should have been the obvious choice.

But Cathy DID insist. My lovely little childhood sweetheart certainly knew what she wanted and was hell-bent on getting married from her mother's home place, and in the same church where her parents were wed twenty-three years earlier. I could just visualize the absolute chaos in that house, at that very moment, with bride and bridesmaids getting into their finery for what I hoped would be Cathy's happiest day.

I didn't really mind where the ceremony took place, provided I got that gold band on her finger. Going for gold at last, after our long stretches apart from each other, with just a little silver claddagh ring to bind us together. It cost all of ten shillings, leaving us without pocket-money at the time. My family knew nothing about Cathy until we began to make preparations. She was my very own secret. We made all sorts of promises to each other when we were in sixth year that one day we would marry, but I almost lost her when I decided to come to Ireland and become a Cockney farmer.

"Go ahead," she stormed, "stick to your flippin' farm. I won't wait around for you." But she did.

Ours was a writing-pad romance. I was good at making up flowery poetry and putting it all down on paper, baring my soul to my one and only. Cathy loved it all, but her old man, a Mayo-man living in London, 'found' a particularly goo-ey twelve-page episode and exploded,

"Is that the sort'a eejit yer thinkin' o'marryin? Smart alecs with'e pen are good for nothin'."

He must have instilled some doubts in her mind. She had practically decided to call off our romance, but after much pleading on my part, and a struggle on hers, we managed to keep it together until she came over to her mothers place in the summer.

I cycled twenty miles on Sunday evenings to see her. Uncle became suspicious when I didn't return until sun-rise, but I just changed into my work-clothes, and got on with the milking, giving him no chance to ask the questions I knew he was longing to fire at me. As he was so fond of saying himself,

"Fotya don't know won't trouble yeh."

So far, Cathy's wishes were all realised, and although I hesitate to say it, if I got MY wish it would be to put Uncle under anaesthetic for at least two days. He was much more concerned about the cows than he was about our wedding.

"Fot if that friesian with'e sore foot don't let down the milk?" he queried. "She might notice yer man strange."

'Yer man' was our next-door neighbour who was obliging enough to take over the milking for the duration of our honey-moon........ a mere three days.

"She can let down what she flippin' likes," I snapped. "Anyone would think I was going away forever."

"It won't be the same again," he muttered sadly, but with a hint of mischief in his eyes that belied his words.

"We'll have a petticoat government from now on. Everthin'll hav'ta be spick an'span. This wan is worshe than yer mother ever was for bossin'."

Actually, he liked Cathy, but he would never admit it. She came to stay with us for a few days in summer and had wrapped him round her little finger in a few hours. He enjoyed his conversations with her so much he said, which was laughable coming from the man who claimed he couldn't understand a word 'them friggin' Cockneys are sayin''.

Mom was teetering around in her new high-heeled shoes, "trying to make the place o'me foot in them," she explained, when I suggested testily that a pair of bleedin' slippers could save breaking her neck on the flag-stone floor. She fussed about, polishing my shoes, ironing my shirts, and brushing my wedding suit, all the while repeating,

"This is the last time I'll do this for yeh," completely forgetting she hadn't performed those tasks for me since I moved to Ireland.

## The Ireland We Remember

Dad scarpered to the local pub with Sean in tow, immediately after breakfast. Which was just as well, considering Uncle's irritating habit of remembering 'to show 'im somethin" in the cow-shed when he was spruced up for the day, and while Dad loved the country-side, he drew a line wherever there was a hint of cowdung. Being such a fastidious man, he reckoned he smelled of it if he just looked at it. I suspected Uncle derived great pleasure from needling him. What was wrong with farm-yard smells, anaway?

I booked the one and only local hackney car to take us to the church. It was spacious enough to accommodate all of us.....or so I hoped......until Mom began shrieking in the back seat,

"Will yeh get up off me skirt. Yer takin' up half the seat."

Uncle was doing just that, with a slight smirk on his face, knowing that Dad......also in the back seat........ would detest any unwanted creases alongside the knife-edge seams in his immaculate black trousers. Mom was sandwiched in the middle, and Sean was squashed between the driver and I in the front seat. After several unsuccessful attempts, when Mom just remembered something, and had to climb over Dad's legs to unlock the front door yet again, the driver finally got started and we rocked and rolled our way down the narrow bumpy boreen. Two miles from the church the car suddenly stopped on the road and refused to budge. The driver listed several good reasons for such a disaster, none of which applied to HIS motor, of course.

"Ah sure, someone'll come along soon an'give us a lift," he comforted me when panic set in.

"Crikey Mike! What the bleedin' 'ell do we do now?" I fumed.

I was so uptight that I was beyond all reasoning. That was Cathy and I finished forever. To be late for one's own wedding was totally unforgivable. I had just decided to start walking when the mail-car......as it was known throughout the county.........spluttered to a halt beside us.

"Trouble?" the postman enquired, noting our new black suits and spanking white shirts.

"Well, we can't letcha get away," he smiled when he realised the problem.

"Hop in the back with'e young lad an' I'll have yeh there in a jiffy. The rest o'ye start walkin' an' someone'll come for ye."

He put us down outside the post-office and arranged for the others to be collected. We all walked to the church door, two hundred yards away, with Mom threatening to 'fling off me high-heels an' go up the chapel in me bare feet'.

Out of the corner of my eye I caught a glimpse of the bride's car.......a shiny black Baby Ford........ winding its way slowly and majestically through the palm-trees. Relief washed over me in great velvety waves, while unmanly tears were perilously close. We all hurried indoors to our seats, making frantic efforts to compose ourselves before Cathy floated up the aisle on her father's arm. Uncle, wiping the sweat off his brow with the back of his hand, remarked jokily,

"Beginners luck, Cockney. Yeh won the last lap."

Everyone said afterwards it was a lovely ceremony, but it was all rather hazy for me except for the moment when I slipped the wedding band on Cathy's finger.

"You're going for gold, Cockney," a little voice sang in my heart.

Nothing else mattered, and the trials and tribulations of the day vanished like mist in the early morning sun. Mountains of food and lashings of drink awaited us at Cathy's ancestral home. The kitchen was cleared for dancing and local lads belted out traditional Irish music. Half-sets and Siege of Ennis were danced with reckless abandon while they shouted wildly,

*"Round the house, an' mind the dhresser."*

Revelry was in the air. Everyone was having a helluva great time. It promised to be a truly unforgettable night. Uncle, fortified with lots of home-brewed mountain dew, was giving a rather unsteady rendition of *'The Rocks of Bawn'* as Cathy and I slipped away quietly to catch the late train to Dublin for our honeymoon...........

*That unforgettable day*

CHAPTER 9

# Cockney's Baby

Uncle was wearing his 'I-know-nothin'' expression at breakfast-time all week. He was a shrewd observer, seeing everything but saying nothing. When he watched Cathy, furtively, out of the corner of his eye, I wanted to snap at him,
"Would you ever mind your own bleedin' business," but I couldn't hurt his feelings, although I sometimes wondered if he had any.

He was so helpful and kind to Cathy ever since she came to Ireland, three years ago, when we got married. He never lost the idiosyncrasies of the old days, but we accepted that, and pulled together, despite getting my back up occasionally with his teasing. He actually beamed when Cathy gave him what he called 'a shnotty answer'. He reckoned she was learning the meaning of 'a sense of humour' at last.

"Them Cockneys over there in *Elephants and Camels* are far too shtuck up," he was fond of reminding her. "They wouldn't see a joke if it hit them between the two eyes."

Well.... Unk would have to wear his 'know-nothin' face for a bit longer. We were not prepared to share our secret with anyone until we were absolutely certain that Cathy was pregnant. Unk would be upfront telling us we were 'a right pair o' eejits' if we got it wrong. I could almost hear him saying, 'better luck next time Cockney'.

Two weeks on, we were in no doubt at all. Cathy was sickly every morning and felt wretched. My heart went out to her, and I wished.... oh, how I wished that I could shoulder all the unpleasantness for her, and see the sparkle in her eyes again. Both of us were a bit nervous. Until recently, we had never really discussed the 'nuts and bolts' of pregnancy, and now, here we were, about to produce our very own 'manufactured in Ireland' baby.

Unk tried to pretend he didn't already guess when we told him our news.

"Jaysus, that's great," he shouted in mock surprise, giving me an almighty wallop on the shoulder. "Another man for the place."

He decided in an instant that it was going to be a boy. Like many men of his time, he believed it was most important to have a son, to ensure the farm was handed down from one generation to the next.

"An' he won't come a minnit too soon," he muttered to no one in particular. "Twenty years from now, that fella there......pointing a finger in my direction......won't be able to do a hand's turn, at the rate he's goin' now."

Crikey! What the heck did he mean? I'd still be in me bleedin' prime, for chris' sake, and I told him so in no uncertain terms. When he could no longer contain himself, he jumped up from his chair, choking with laughter, and made for the door, spluttering and spitting as he coughed out,

"God, it's fierce aisy to rattle yeh, Cockney, yeh haven't learned a thing."

I could have kicked myself for falling into the old familiar trap. Uncle was a dab hand at windin' people up. We knew in our hearts he was almost as excited as we were ourselves, and he became over protective of Cathy as time progressed, insisting on what she should or should not do. She could swing her leg over the bar of my bike like any young tomboy, and streak to the village for a few groceries, with long brown hair flying in the summer breeze, and freckles appearing on her arms from the warm sun.

But, Unk was having no more of that. He decided to buy her a girl's bike, which must have been painful, as he was not easily separated from his money. He built a broad 'step' with sods of turf, at the gable of the house, and leaned the new bike against it. Cathy was instructed to step up carefully and sit on the saddle, then pedal away slowly, 'an' sthop actin' like a tearaway'. I dreaded the day when he might consider mounting his own oul' 'crock' to escort her to the shop or Sunday Mass, but, thankfully, it never happened.

For Cathy and I, the days sped by with alarming rapidity. Our time alone together seemed to be confined to bed-time when we cuddled up closely and shared our dreams and our hopes for our baby. We tried, in vain, to select a name. Cathy made a long list of boy/girl names, but we decided that none of them would befit this gorgeous, wonderful, never-seen-before tiny miracle.

For Unk, the time crawled at a maddening snails pace. He was like a youngster waiting for something nice to happen. When he had a few pints inside his shirt on a Saturday night in the pub, he proudly announced to all and sundry,

"We're goin' to have a son," and the oul' fellas smiled and remarked,

"Aisy known yeh never had childher o'yer own."

Sometime into the eighth month of Cathy's pregnancy, Unk became very busy in the barn for long periods. We knew he was working with timber, but the job was shrouded in mystery until one day he invited us to come and admire his handywork. Cathy gasped when she saw the cradle he had produced. It was rough and it was tough, "but that young lad won't put his foot through it in a hurry," he assured us, with chest-swelling pride. Cathy was livid. Did he really believe we would put our precious infant into a monstrosity like that? She stormed out of the barn in anger.

Somewhat chastened by her outburst, he admitted, reluctantly, that in his over-enthusiastic mood he neglected to plane the timber sufficiently to get a nice smooth surface.

"Nothin' wrong that can't be put right," he muttered in aggrieved tones, and two days later we were admiring a superb piece of carpentry, mounted on rockers, and all the timber, as he put it himself, 'as smooth as a baby's bottom'.

"It's a cradle fit for that crowd in the palace," he announced grandly.

Even Cathy had to agree.

Not surprisingly, my jocose uncle was steeped in superstition, No way would that cradle be allowed into the house until it was actually needed. Baby must arrive first, he insisted. Afterwards, the cradle would be placed near the fire 'to give it a good warmin' up before yer man is put into it'.

His displeasure was obvious when Cathy's mother, Molly, arrived from London for this momentous occasion, bringing with her a huge bag of baby-clothes and toys, but Unk was unimpressed.

"That's the sorta nonsense that brings bad luck into a house," he muttered crossly.

But my feisty, fifty-something mother-in-law, being Irish herself, and no stranger to superstition, promptly dismissed it all as 'a load of oul' *sheafóid*'.

He turned his attention to me Mom, then,

"If tha' wan is comin' over, she'll havta shleep in the carthouse. We're overcrowded here as we are...," he muttered, with a sidelong glance at an outraged Cathy. His look clearly indicated his dislike of intrusive females, at this emotional time in particular.

When Cathy woke early one morning with minor tummy aches that gradually developed into labour pains, I almost panicked. Unk was a nervous wreck altogether. I fervently wished he would go to the cowshed and start the milking. Even when he shaved he nicked a piece off his jaw and his ear, and had blood spattered all over his shirt collar.

Cathy was giving birth at home, like all the young mothers of that time. I grabbed my bike and pedalled furiously to our local doctor's house, throwing pebbles at his top window in a frenzied effort to wake him up quickly......

One hour later, when my fingers ached with nail-biting, that infuriatingly calm and composed doctor placed an adorable baby girl in Cathy's eager arms. Suddenly, I was both crying and laughing with heaven-sent palpable relief that mother and baby were safe.

Unk was slightly taken aback at first, but one peep at the new-born infant, and all thoughts of 'a man for the place' were put on hold.

The strain of the previous hours was obvious. I was cackling like an over-excited old woman, holding the baby unsteadily, with tears of joy creating a big damp patch on Cathy's shoulder. This precious little bundle was all ours, and we would never cease to be amazed at the wonder of it all.

Molly finally persuaded Unk to 'lave them to it' and both retired to the kitchen 'to wet the baby's head'.

Several drinks later, Unk was singing *The Rocks of Bawn* at the top of his voice, dimly aware that Cockney would have lots to say when there wasn't a cow milked 'at that hour o' the day' while Molly, not to be outdone, stepped giddily around the floor, pretending to hold the baby, and crooned softly,

*'She's a pretty little girl from Cunga in the county of Mayo'.*

# The Ireland We Remember

*A baby brings joy*

## CHAPTER 10

# Home to Mayo

WOODHOUNDS, THE VILLAGE WHERE I was born and reared. I must have said the name aloud dozens of times as I drove from Shannon to Mayo in the early morning sunshine. Woodhounds had occupied my mind totally for weeks. I was going home for the first time in years, and the prospect was exhilarating.

I had never been particularly interested in the old homestead, tucked away in sheltered seclusion, at the foot of the hill, but providing an excellent view of the surrounding farms from the front door. Recently, for some inexplicable reason, I was consumed with an incredible longing to see the place just once, before ……..before the chip on my shoulder embittered me for life, although I would never admit it. Before my parents passed on, I told myself. At which precise moment I was unexpectedly and acutely aware that they could have long since crossed the Jordan in my absence.

My mother would be sixty-four now, and my father must be seventy. They looked old when I was a boy. Both of them would probably be using walking canes at this stage, I reflected, assuming they were still around. Pushing aside those morose thoughts, I began to whistle *'Moonlight in Mayo'* as the car ate up the miles between me and Woodhounds.

Would I be able to endure the sort of lifestyle I remembered so well, even for a brief three-week vacation? No running water. An outdoor toilet.....maybe. No mod cons of any kind.

At nineteen I couldn't wait to get away from it all. Twenty years in America, sweating it out, year after year, chasing the mighty dollar. Urged on by the dream of so many emigrants – to make good, and return to Ireland one day.

How often I recalled the words of an old neighbour, the day I left home. Tears were streaming down my mother's cheeks as I waved her goodbye and old Ned next door shook my hand and said with conviction,

"You'll come back, son. The savage loves his native land."

I was full of conviction. "Look, give me five years," I told anyone who wanted to listen, "and I'll be a self-made man."

Hearing my father's snort of disbelief in the background, hostility flared once again and I snapped furiously,

"I'll be back, but not to squelch in the muck all day like you. I'm going to make it big. You wait and see."

It was so much easier said than done. The early days were interlaced with a fierce determination to succeed, and moments of overwhelming desire to return. Then I remembered my father's scepticism and got down to work. Every task was executed with ruthless efficiency. My father would have been very surprised indeed if he could have seen me six months later. Initially I was adamant that I would return 'noveau riche' and show them all what decent living was like. Especially my father who was content to live in his little thatched cottage surrounded by his sheep and his pigs.

I was not the son he had hoped for. The spade and the shovel were not for me. My younger brother, Billy, was welcome to them, if he was damn fool enough to stay. But I had other objectives. Accumulating dollars became an obsession and I certainly realised my ambition as the five years spread into ten. Sadly, in the intervening years thoughts of returning to my native land were deferred to the hazy distant future.

My heart said,

"You promised, go home and see them," but my head replied, "Don't spend your hard earned dollars."

At first I wrote to my mother occasionally but gradually lost interest in the long epistles of home events, which she mailed with unfailing regularity. The thoughts of writing home became such an ordeal that eventually my half page of impossible-to-write rubbish was consigned to the litter bin forever. From thereon, all communication with home ceased. I moved from one city to the next, never leaving a forwarding address. I worked extremely hard, rising each morning with the prayer,

'Another day, another dollar'.

Sometimes I thought about my mother and was ridden with guilt on seeing her face, sad and lonely, despairing of ever hearing from her first-born again. What will she think of me now, I wondered, as I wound my way round the numerous hair-pin bends on the quiet country roads in my rented car. She always told me I was a 'real-good looker' in the old days, and I was still a tall, virile, dark-haired, athletic looking guy.

'*O take me back to Mayo*' my heart sang, noting the 'Welcome to Mayo' road sign, which told me I was almost there.

I didn't consider it necessary to send advance warning of my impending arrival. Secretly, I wanted to soak up the amazement on their faces, when I drove up to the half-door.

Cars would still be a rarity around Woodhounds, I presumed. I was about to strut my stuff.

I ground the car to a halt in consternation. Where was the cart-house? "I don't believe this" I muttered in dismay. The thatched cottage was no more. In its place stood a modern bungalow, with its neat tarmacadam driveway and a well-dented Vauxhall parked carelessly outside the front door.

"What the heck," I thought angrily. "Are that shower all dead and gone? This place gotta belong to some other folk now."

In my heart I could see my mother plodding along to the pig-house with two buckets of swill, as I had seen her do so many times in my childhood. I hated it then. Why did I expect her to carry on doing it all those years, and at this moment in particular? Why did I assume that nothing would alter until I decided to return?

Suddenly my thoughts were interrupted as my father came across from the barn at the rear of the house. Yes – that was him. As long and as lean as ever. Still straight as a whip. There was very little change, except for the fact that his hair was no longer quite as coal-black as I remembered. The years rolled away as he shook my hand unemotionally, and said,

"Huh! Yeh came back, did yeh?" Then he looked skywards and said the same words I had heard him say countless times in the past, "There's rain on it."

I knew I was home.

"We'll be going to Mass soon," he told me as we walked towards the front door of the imposing new bungalow. "Will yeh ..." he looked at me hesitantly.

Shaking my head, I replied mockingly, "You're not carrying on with that crap still are you?"

"Like my motor?" I asked changing the subject as we walked.

Carefully removing his pipe, he said slowly.

"Ach, I don't know, I think I'd rather that oul' yoke at the door. Yeh wouldn't get lost in it, d'yeh see."

So much for having chosen the biggest car I could cope with, solely to impress.

Just then my mother came running to the door. "I heard voices," she began, breaking off as incredulous joy lit up her face. Is she really my mother, I asked myself as I hugged her tightly and then held her away from me to look at her some more. Who was this snappy dresser with the soft wavy brown hair? Where was my badly dressed mousey-looking mother gone to? How was she managing to stand upright in those trendy high heels?

"Just while I'm at Mass," she laughed as she caught my glance. "They match my suit. We like to dress up in this part of the world," she added looking disdainfully at my grubby T-shirt and shorts.

"Twenty years gone and he still can't afford a trouser," my father muttered to no one in particular.

Noting my displeasure, my mother sent a cautious glance in my father's direction and effectively diffused the situation by saying lightly,

"Don't look so serious, son. Sure we don't give a hoot if you go around in your pelt." Winding her arms about my waist, she whispered softly, "It's good to see you Mickie. You're home at last."

Mickie Sullivan. The boy name. I had forgotten that. I'd been Michael O'Sullivan since I left home. It was comforting to be enfolded in my mother's arms. I was feeling like a child again, loved and secure.

"You lucky son-of-a-bitch," I scolded myself, making a mental note not to indulge in vulgar language in Woodhounds. "You've given them hell all those years, with your silence, and they're happy to have you back."

My mellow mood remained with me for just a few minutes. Then memories of other days came flooding back and

## The Ireland We Remember

once again I could hear my father calling me a 'good-for-nothin'' while my mother urged me to 'do somethin' right, sometime, an' stop vexin' 'im'.

"Ye'll see the day when ye won't be fit to lick my boots," I had screamed at him, still at that age when a lambasting from my father could hurt severely, and tears could flow piteously. Oh God, why couldn't I let go and put the past where it well and truly deserved to be? It was time to get rid of all the suppressed anger in my system forever.

Soon I was tucking into a huge breakfast of bacon and eggs. Where else did bacon taste like it did in Woodhounds? Where else did brown bread look so inviting? Dear Lord, it was good to be home. For years, my breakfast consisted of black coffee swallowed hastily as I drove to work. I shuddered in distaste now.

Nothing would induce my mother to miss her Sunday morning Mass, even on the coldest days, and my unheralded arrival was no deterrent. These guys are hell-bent on handing out surprises, I thought, as she got behind the Vauxhall's steering wheel and reversed smartly round the corner of the house.

"Are yeh comin'?" she asked, while my father settled himself in the passenger seat.

"You must be joking," I laughed, turning to go indoors.

"Billy is out in the fields," she called, hurt in her eyes.

"He'll be goin' to late Mass," she added as she sped down the old road to the village chapel.

Mass. It was a long time since I had served Mass in that little chapel. I didn't intend to get religious now. I did fine without all that crap for years, but perhaps I'd have a quick look inside, just for old time's sake. Nothing more.

I arrived a few minutes late in my good suit and white shirt. My tie was choking me. I hadn't worn one in a long time. I knelt inside the door and was immediately enveloped in the peace and tranquillity which permeated the building.

'*Nearer my God to thee*' floated down from the choir on the gallery, and for the first time in twenty years I whispered the words 'Hail Mary, full of Grace' as I gazed at the old familiar statue of the Virgin Mary, still standing to the left of the High Altar.

After Mass the men congregated outside under the big yew tree just as they did in my youth. I had vivid memories of diving in and out between them, making futile efforts to sell the 'Catholic Standard' for the local curate.

There were many more surprises in store. Billy was married to Agnes Daly from a neighbouring village, and had a ten-year old son and twin daughters of nine. Aggie, whom I damn well recognised but pretended otherwise. I had never forgotten the scorn on her face when I tried to date her.

"Them oul' fellas think they've got it all," she told her friend, tossing her heavy mane of blonde hair. I was eighteen and it stung.

"Dammit man, you cannot all be living under the one roof," I exploded as the family picture unfolded over Sunday lunch. Aggie spoke clearly and resolutely for the first time.

"We can and we are. Your Mom and Dad are part of our family and we wouldn't be without them." Fixing me with her steady gaze she added. "There's still room for anyone who cares to climb down from their lofty perch and stay with us for a week or two or three. Everyone is welcome in this house."

For some perverse reason I knocked every word they said as they updated me with the farm's progress in my absence. Everything was bigger and better in America I told them. I extolled the delights of my luxury 'condo', carefully concealing the fact that I was painfully aware of what overcrowding in a house meant. Eight men in one room. Bearable, if they were clean, but bloody awful when the stench of sweat and dirty socks spiralled from the beds in the hot summers. I had grown accustomed to spartan living of an extreme kind when I first left home, but my family would never know that. I had become silent and withdrawn, yearning for the day I could afford a place of my own. Now at thirty-nine, I realised I had almost forgotten what it was like to be young. Forgotten what it was like to smile and joke a lot, like my brother Billy, who at thirty five was so light-hearted and happy, looking as if he had never stepped out of his teens.

Apparently I'd been remarkably ill-informed over the years. On the rare occasions when I roused myself to ask some acquaintance,

"How're things in the oul' sod?" on discovering he'd been back to see his folks, I invariably got the standard answer,

"Same as ever. Nothing changes over there."

How wrong. How very, very wrong. Only a few hours home and already I could see the changes. Ireland had progressed well in twenty years and I resented that progress. I wanted to brag about Uncle Sam, who was, undoubtedly very good to me. I hoped to tell them what life in the fast lane was all about, of which I was convinced they knew nothing. I also had the urge to hit out and prove that they were still living in the thirties, while I was living out there in the fifties. I had worried myself sick wondering how I'd manage when nature called. I intended to bang my fist on the table and rudely tell my father,

"Dammit man, you don't even have running water over here."

They had. They had everything, and their hearts were as big as their bodies, as I discovered long before my three weeks vacation was over. As the days passed, the unwelcome discovery that I was the one who needed to be pitch-forked into the fifties was disquieting indeed.

It was with great reluctance that I boarded the plane at Shannon for my return flight to America. I had one definite plan in mind. Within the year I would return to Woodhounds and build my own bungalow. Perhaps I would marry one day. I was still a tall, dark, handsome thirty-niner! Thanks to Uncle Sam I could relax and think about the girls now ….. someone like Aggie, who was still a stunningly beautiful blonde at thirty-four. I was still wallowing in the stuff that dreams are made of, when the pilot's voice announced,

"We will be landing at Kennedy Airport in fifteen minutes. Please fasten your seatbelts and remain seated …."

*Beautiful familiar countryside*

CHAPTER 11

# Some Aunts Do Have It

AUNT SARAH WAS AT it again. She never lost an opportunity to try a bit of matchmaking on behalf of her niece during her annual visits to the old homestead.

"Leave well enough alone," her brother muttered when she sought his advice about her plans for Kate.

"The Man above will take care of her in His own good time," he remarked lazily.

"Anyway, don't we all know marriages are made in heaven," he added, winking wickedly.

"Absolute rubbish," Sarah retorted her voice loaded with scepticism. "You don't need to go anywhere near Heaven. Joe and I were living proof of that."

Her voice broke, suddenly tearful. She steadfastly believed that marriages were made aboard luxury liners, for the very good reason that many years ago she set sail from Cobh on the Cunard Liner, and met the love of her life on the six-week voyage to America. She married him shortly after going ashore in New York and never once regretted it.

Despite her brother's reluctance to meddle in his daughter's affairs, Sarah forged ahead with her scheme and invited Kate to accompany her on a three-week luxury cruise from San Francisco to Alaska. The prospect of going to California was greeted by Kate with excitement and enthusiasm, and scant regard for Aunt Sarah's plans to get her off the shelf before her 'sell-by' date. She was only too familiar with her aunt's efforts at match-making on her frequent journeys back to 'th' oul' sod'. She dictated their lives when she came home, and Kate and her sisters did their own thing when she left.

However, if Aunt Sarah wished to give the old match-making routine another whirl, Kate was happy to oblige - for the moment. After all, who in their right mind would decline the offer of a visit to California with a three-week luxury cruise included? In all of her twenty-five years Kate had never been out of Ireland and this was indeed a heaven-sent opportunity. Never mind Aunt Sarah's plans for her future. She would cross those bridges later, she decided.

Money was no problem for her aunt. She spared no expense to groom Kate for this great adventure, suggesting that she arrive in San Francisco 'in the clothes she stood up in'. Aunt Sarah belonged to the generation who believed Ireland never moved forward, and if Kate did have clothes they would be totally unsuitable to wear when they met this wonder-man they would most assuredly find before the cruise ended.

Kate gasped in amazement when her Aunt took her down to see The Princess, moored at Fisherman's Wharf, awaiting her journey to Alaska. The magnitude and the splendour of this majestic lady, so passive in the tranquil waters of the bay, was a joy to behold. Kate couldn't take it all in. San Francisco at night had to be seen to be believed, and The Princess enhanced the wonder and the magic.

They sailed with five hundred passengers on board, all eager to sample the delights of luxury living. Aunt Sarah explained patiently that you eat and you drink when Kate enquired, rather naively, what they did on board ship. One thing Aunt Sarah had in common with all the other passengers was her passion for food - loads of rich saucy foods, beautifully served by smartly-dressed, silent-footed waiters in the magnificent dining room of The Princess. She indulged her habit with reckless abandon, totally oblivious of her ample proportions and her three chins.

Kate had never worn an evening gown in her life. Nice dresses, yes. Real, real evening gowns, no. She was painfully conscious of what she referred to as her semi-nudity when they entered the ballroom each night. Aunt Sarah had no such qualms. She floated around with a drink in hand, displaying acres of sun-tanned flesh, while she tapped her feet invitingly, ever ready to take the floor when the band began to play.

Fortunately for Kate, she herself was a reasonably good dancer and had no shortage of partners. She was too happy to care whether they were young or old. On reflection they were neither. Most were middle-aged, well-fed, fun-loving men and Kate glided from one to the other like the Cinderella that she was.

Occasionally, Aunt Sarah looked on disapprovingly. She wanted action, not this flitting around like a butterfly. She expected hearts to be splintering all over the ballroom. Didn't they know Kate was her niece, for goodness sake? Could they not see that she was young, pretty, single and available? However, her spirits lifted as she remembered her own progress with Senator Markham. He was her constant companion since they came aboard. Such beautiful old world manners too.

They sailed farther north each day, past Eureka, Gold Beach, Willapa Bay and Grey's Harbour. Kate never knew that such luxury existed, and never realised that people had such extravagant tastes. The ladies were beautifully groomed and expensively attired. The men looked exactly what they were - wealthy tycoons enjoying a break.

When they eventually went ashore in Seattle for thirty-six hours, most people on board were aware that Aunt Sarah had entered Kate for the 'Matrimonial Stakes'. Most people also could see at a glance that Kate 'was refusing the jumps' as one nice horsey lady remarked with great amusement. Nobody cared. They were all having a wonderful cruise, and a little match-making added 'spice' to their idyllic holiday. One friendly fleshy man with whiskey-laden breath told Kate huskily,

"You don't get serious on these cruises, honey-babe. Just allow yourself to get carried away, but never too far to return unscathed."

Kate's sentiments exactly. She loved him for the remainder of the voyage.

There was much excitement and expectancy when they sighted Alaska days later. While The Princess nudged her way into Glacier Bay, cameras clicked all around as people pressed forward to get their first pictures of the world-famous glaciers. Laughter bubbled up inside Kate as Senator Markham adjusted Aunt Sarah's camera strap around her neck, affording her much unnecessary assistance while she so obviously enjoyed his closeness.

They drank ale in The Red Onion Saloon in Skagway, or huge mugs of black coffee, and pizzas according to their variable moods. They visited The Brass Pic with its historic Crib, where the warning sign over the low door said 'Duck it or knock it'. They visited every gift-shop and explored every conceivable place of interest until traces of exhaustion began to overtake Aunt Sarah. She retired to her cabin for a day, relaxing totally as The Princess swayed gently to and fro in the bay, and after an earlier-than-usual night in bed she had found her sea legs again.

There was so much to do and see throughout the day, and so many new friends to talk to. Kate sat with her aunt on the sun-deck in a vain attempt to slow her pace, if only for a brief period. They looked out over the Pacific and soaked up the sun while they sipped their iced drinks. Occasionally Kate joined with others for a game of tennis and cooled off afterwards in the pool, always under the watchful eye of Aunt Sarah who wanted romance rather than racquets.

The male sun-worshippers on the deck were not quite Kate's type after all, Sarah decided, as her exhaustion began to disappear rapidly, to be replaced by a sudden burst of energy. She would have Kate back in the ballroom after dinner. Men were at their most romantic after a good rich meal, accompanied by a few brandies, or her name was not Sarah Murphy. Thereafter, everyone enjoyed the sentimental music and song in the ballroom. Who could fail to be smitten by Kate, looking so pretty in her beautiful gown as they danced dreamily to the strains of 'Love Thee Dearest' at midnight? If only Kate would show a little interest instead of flitting around like a bee at a honey-pot. Sarah sighed in mild frustration.

The highlight of their return journey was dinner at the Captain's table on their last night at sea. Aunt Sarah positively glowed as the Captain took her outstretched hands, welcoming her like an old and valued friend while he escorted her to his table with the Senator close behind. Later, when they managed to be all alone the Senator suggested they retire to the deck to discuss plans for a subsequent cruise, and next morning Kate purposely turned a blind eye as she observed their emotional and loving farewells before finally going ashore.

The sheer affluence and reckless self-indulgence on this wonderful, unforgettable cruise would remain with Kate forever. But now Ireland beckoned. Soon she would be back to bacon and cabbage and stainless steel cutlery. Dinner tables adorned with costly silver and ornate crystal goblets would be just beautiful, lingering, treasured memories.

*Fishermans Wharf in San Francisco*

CHAPTER 12

# Sauce for the Goose

It was the day that was in it that made it so memorable. Or more accurately, it was the handsome hunk standing at the bar in a green jacket, sporting a yellow tie spattered with shamrocks that made it so unforgettable. Amy could see little bits of him in the mirror behind the bottles of dry gin and earnestly wished he would turn around and show his face. He did...... eventually, and she was not disappointed. He was simply gorgeous. Tall, dark-haired and prosperous looking with a cigar dangling between his teeth .... and he was alone. He wasn't fair and handsome like the man of her dreams. His rugged features and curly black hair, together with a pair of piercing brown eyes, gave him a sort of Latin look, she decided. But it wouldn't matter provided he had money....loads of the stuff. Amy was intrigued from that very moment.

She was a vivacious twenty-one year old, with fair shoulder length hair, flicked out at the ends. She had beautiful laughter-filled blue eyes, and her pithy humour and infectious happy grin were like a tonic. You could be forgiven for immediately thinking of 'Babycham' from the bubble and sparkle which emanated from her, and she could be relied upon one hundred per cent to get into mischief wherever she went.

Twelve months earlier, she had secured a job as an Au Pair to a wealthy business family in New York.Their one and only little girl, whom Amy promptly decided 'badly needed remodelling', was in her charge, and with her Irish luck holding all the way, she set about moulding the child into a nice friendly little youngster, far removed from the spoiled brat she took over when she first arrived.

The Jefferson family just loved Amy. Were all the Irish so effervescent, they wondered, delighted to be fortunate enough to have found such a treasure. Their house abounded with love and joy and their little girl blossomed.

"It's a great day for the Irish," some 'wino' sang loudly into his green beer at the other end of the bar.

"It will be, n'all, when Pierce Brosnan looks in our direction," Amy whispered excitedly to her friend Bridget. St. Patrick's Day was still young, and it would be no fault of hers if he wasn't sitting at their table before the day ended. Ever since leaving school, Amy had one goal in mind… to marry a man with money. Not for her the scrimping and scraping like her parents way back in the west of Ireland. Money spoke volumes. Money glossed over most of life's little pinpricks and to date Amy's life was porous with pinpricks of all sorts, mainly financial ones. She had always heard that you had to 'have money to meet money' and now she was about to experiment with 'what's on the other side'.

Barry's gaze roamed idly over the patrons of Sullivan's Bar, lingering lazily over some of the girls, before moving on and finally coming to rest on Amy's petite figure and very pretty face. He could read the body language clearly, and

## The Ireland We Remember

minutes later he picked up his glass and moved towards their table.

"I'm Barry," he said by way of introduction, "You guys fancy another beer?"

They did. They had several, while the most colourful parade in the world marched through the streets of New York.

Amy's granny always said 'beer loosened the tongue,' and she was probably right. Barry filled in his background for his gobsmacked listeners ....... very well-to-do family. His father was an investment banker in the city and owned a country mansion in Westchester County, which would belong to Barry one day, and to which his family retreated at week-ends to get away from it all. Amy could see herself settling into this lifestyle. That there was no shortage of dollars was evident, but such a delicate subject was not up for discussion on this great occasion.

"Enough about me. Tell me what you guys do," he suggested tactfully.

Amy beamed. Her acting abilities went into overdrive immediately. "Why be a humble au pair when I can be the daughter of the big house instead," she thought gleefully.

To Bridget's acute embarrassment, Amy elaborated at great length about her Irish ancestors who emigrated to the U.S.A over two hundred years ago, and wistfully confided her secret dream of finding her roots one day. She excelled herself with her American accent, injecting just the slightest trace of Irish in readiness for a possible slip-up.

"Great Grandpa made his pile working on the railroads in West Virginia. We owe him a debt of gratitude for all we have to-day," she recounted with great modesty.

She felt no need to mention that she was simply an au pair for a wealthy American couple, with a young child, in upstate New York, or the fact that she sought employment there to earn enough money to pursue her acting career at drama school. It was a tribute to her excellent acting that Barry accepted her story without question. He was most impressed with her wide and knowledgeable views on farming and indeed all subjects Irish, handed down by her ancestors and endorsed by her Irish nanny of course. Amy giggled. Wasn't she up to her ankles in muck every time she stepped outside the backyard at home. If anyone was a connoisseur of farming she certainly was. Barry was totally fascinated by the muted Irish pronunciation of some of her words, and said so.

"Blame my Irish nanny for that," she lied innocently, "she lived with us for ten years."

"Gee, honey, that's cute," Barry exclaimed in admiration. "You sure got yourself one heck of an Irish twang."

Bridget almost choked on her bottle o' 'Buds'.

And I'm not doing too bad myself, he thought smugly. He couldn't believe his luck. Amy would be the fulfilment of his dreams. Not only was she 'flush', she was stunningly beautiful also. Here was one little jewel he was going to hold on to at all costs.

Everyone wore green and sang Irish songs throughout the afternoon and night. Baskets of 'crubeens' were there for the taking at the bar counter. Dinners of bacon and cabbage were served, and eaten with relish. No one thought of going home. The 'craic' was mighty.

Amy had a long train-ride back to Mount Kisco afterwards. In the morning she would relay the days events to her very interested employers, and she'd tell them all about Barry, she decided drowsily, climbing into bed at three in the morning......

Jack Barry drove to work early. This was the time of year he made his money. March was the month for frozen pipes, burst pipes, no water, and central heating refusing to function. God, his head was bursting too. He'd get an aspirin from Mrs. Jefferson before he commenced work in that damp basement of hers. She was a great one for 'the cure'. Jack was hazy about the day before, but......if an Irishman couldn't drown the shamrock in the Big Apple......who could? He was vaguely aware of talking too much, but his companions were so vivacious and so voluble it was easy to get caught up in their geniality........

Amy was preparing breakfast for her young protégé when she heard a muttered oath. Beside her stood Barry, a dull red colour creeping up his face. Clarity returned with a bang. This was the little beauty whose Grandpa worked on the railroads, looking defiant, yet bewitching. His speech deserted him. Hostility flared, but subsided almost instantly. Who was he to pass judgement? He made a right eejit of himself last night.

"So.... you're the au pair Mrs. Jefferson has been on about," he managed at last shamefacedly.

"And you must be Jack Barry, the Irish plumber she's expecting this morning," Amy flung back.

"The same Jack Barry, no doubt, who updated all the antiquated plumbing in this place three years ago."

"He's such a honey," she mimicked Mrs. Jefferson perfectly, "I just love him."

He looked so repentant that Amy burst into helpless laughter, and taking courage he said sheepishly,

"Could we put this behind us and start afresh?"

Amy agreed readily. After all, he was the most gorgeous hunk she ever met in her life.

# Anne Morrin

*Drowning the Shamrock in New York*

CHAPTER 13

# From Riches to Rags

Lady Georgina Crofton-Carew was a rich woman. She was her stupendously wealthy grandfather's sole heiress, and while that man had a wholesome respect for money, it was a trait he failed to instil in his capricious granddaughter. My acquaintance with 'Lady G', as she was affectionately known to all, went back three years - to the summer of 1948 in fact, when she became a frequent visitor to the hotel over-looking Lough Corrib where I was employed as a housemaid.

Ladies and lords, owners of huge mansions and vast acres of land were not at all unusual in those days, and the west held a certain magnetic attraction for most of them. They returned year after year for the mayfly fishing, and later for the dapping season. With numerous salmon, trout, and pike-fishing lakes to choose from, they certainly enjoyed their holidays in the quiet backwater of Mayo.

Lady G. was passionately fond of fishing and made frequent visits to indulge in her favourite pastime. Each morning she donned her bright yellow oilskins and sou'wester to head for the boathouse where her ghillie awaited her with his boat. They set forth with an incredible assortment of fishing tackle to catch 'the big one' in the nearby waters of the lake.

She was both extravagant and generous with everyone around her. A most vivacious and witty lady whose ample figure spoke of self-indulgence. She dressed carelessly, rarely styled her soft brown hair, smoked endless cigarettes and drank with reckless abandon. The hotel staff were the recipients of her lavish generosity. She was an immensely popular woman with a heart as big as her body. Everyone received a tip when she was leaving. Small wonder that we all looked forward so eagerly to her visits. We were not the only ones. There was never a shortage of friends prepared to accompany her on her many fishing trips. Secretly we dubbed them 'The bees around the honey-pot'.

Lady G's passion for entertaining almost equalled that of her passion for fishing, and her beautiful north County Dublin mansion was a hive of activity with unfailing regularity. She had a most efficient staff in whom she could place absolute trust to take care of every detail, both in her presence and her absence.

Perhaps no one was more surprised than I was when she said casually one morning, with a cigarette dangling from her mouth, and ash all over the bedroom carpet,

"How would you like to come and work for me, child"?

How would I like to work for her? How I would love it! I was as eager as any other eighteen-year old to venture out and explore, but how could I leave my secure job in the hotel? My contribution to the family finances was needed where my parents lived in their little thatched cottage on the rugged edge of the Atlantic. Lady G. took care of all that. An expert in the art of manipulation, she quickly convinced my somewhat dubious mother that I should 'go out into the world' and 'be educated'.

A considerable sum of money changed hands with great delicacy while she assured her repeatedly that I would be in her own safe hands. Soothing words were poured into the hotel manager's ear when he tut-tutted about staff leaving in mid-season, and he also received a very acceptable handshake for his understanding and co-operation. One week later, I was whisked away in a chauffeur-driven limousine to Lady G's magnificent residence on the outskirts of Dublin.

I was happy enough in my new job. Cook and the gardener were like family, and if at times I longed to hear the waves pounding on the shore and feel the soft sand under my bare feet, I quickly suppressed those feelings. I missed the piercing cries of the seagulls as they wheeled round and round overhead in the marsh that separated us from the sea. I never tired of looking out on the Atlantic where the waves foamed and frothed with anger when seas were rough. The same seas that caressed the rocks leaving a velvety sheen on their surface on long hot summer days. I knew an overwhelming sense of loneliness if I dwelt on it for long.

Life continued comfortably until persistent nagging doubts began to invade my mind, like ominous clouds before a storm. Lady G. usually took me shopping with her, and I watched in stunned silence as she engaged in petty thieving each time we entered a store. Convincing myself that she was absent-minded, or as my Father would say, 'goin' a bitteen *seafóideach'*, I would urge her to pay but to my dismay she would snap,

"Just mind your own business, child. When I want your advice I'll ask for it," and I would edge towards the exit with a hammering heart.

Over a period of time the 'little things' became 'big things', and I lived in constant fear of detection. Eventually the dreaded day came. With churning stomach and sweaty palms I was marched along with Lady G. to the store-manager's office, to watch her go down the long road of humiliation and pain.

Later at a court hearing, words that I did not understand, like 'kleptomaniac' and 'personality disorders' were floating around between her lawyer and doctor. They pleaded hard for her, stressing the need for medical attention, but the judge was adamant. My heart wept for her that day. She seemed to age prematurely as she grasped the words 'Three months'. She received a horrendous body blow when she was jailed for theft. Nothing could have prepared her for her shock in having to swop her opulent life-style for the austerity of prison life.

Three months stretched endlessly before her horrified eyes as she was led away in an agony of despair. She had been preparing for an extra special Christmas celebration that year, and the staff were already painting the rooms in the east wing to accommodate her overseas guests. Now her plans lay in ruins around her. She was totally devastated. Cook sent me to visit her occasionally in prison.

"A young thing like you will cheer her up," she told me, but I doubted the wisdom of her words.

Never in my young life had I seen such utter dejection or change of personality. She vented her anger on me suggesting I could have averted this ignominy.

"Get the hell out of here," she would scream.

"Bloody culchie. Go home to your hens and chickens in Connemara. I'm sick of you."

Next time she would be full of apologies and remorse.

"Bear with me, love," she would sob piteously with tears streaming down her lined face.

But it never lasted. She became more despondent with each day. It hurt unbearably to see the despair in her eyes, but when she hurled abuse and shouted,

## The Ireland We Remember

"Don't come sneaking in here again, you damned little country bumpkin," my control would almost snap. Instantly I would recall her generous and loving nature, and silently declare undying loyalty to this unfortunate and unhappy woman suffering enormous mental torture.

Worse was in store. Her financial affairs were in total disarray. Circumstances compelled her to dispose of most of her estate to defray the costs of insolvency. Where are all her friends now I wondered, when most of her magnificent furniture was auctioned and carried away by proud new owners.

Three months dragged by and at last the intolerable sentence was over. Lady G. was released two days before Christmas. She was overjoyed. Cook and the gardener and I scurried around putting up Christmas decorations and re-arranging the remaining pieces of furniture in the semi-empty rooms.

Despite our best efforts we felt it would be a bleak Christmas for her. The long and impressive guest list drawn up with such care in August was now obsolete. One by one the little regret notes came through the letterbox, and we realised her friends were fair-weather ones after all. We need not have worried. Lady G. waved her hand dismissively and told us bluntly she didn't give a damn about the land - or the furniture.

"I'll have Christmas dinner with all of you at the kitchen table," she announced decisively. "We're going to have a lovely day."

She was home. To adjust to a lifestyle in total contrast to her former one. She gathered us around her, her eyes suddenly misty with unshed tears, and her heart quite obviously filled to overflowing.

"Thank you, my really genuine friends," she said, her voice hoarse with emotion.

"How fortunate I am to have you. We'll no longer be well off, but we'll survive. With friends like you who needs riches?"

"Happy Christmas, Lady G.," I ventured hesitantly, moving towards her with outstretched hand.

For an answer, she enfolded me in her arms and with a wealth of love and tenderness in her voice, and a twinkle in her eye, she whispered softly,

"And Happy Christmas to you too, my much loved country bumpkin."

*Riches cannot buy me love*

CHAPTER 14

# Paddie's Man

BILLY MURPHY DUG HIS spade into the ground as the last green sod was pressed down on his grandmother's grave, and joined with the large gathering of people to say a final farewell to a great lady. Old Sarah Cavanagh passed away in her sleep two days before at the advanced age of one hundred and two years, and they had just now laid her to rest in the local graveyard beside the church where she worshiped throughout her entire life. In keeping with tradition, all the relatives, neighbours, gravediggers, half the parish made their way afterwards to the village pub to have 'the last one on Sarah', paying glowing tributes to a vivacious and sprightly woman who was all things to all the neighbours for many years.

Sarah arranged her funeral with care and attention. Ample funds were set aside from thirty years of old age pension for a 'decent wake' and a 'respectable burial'. She insisted that all who came to pay their respects be treated to generous measures of poteen and whiskey and they in turn obligingly respected her wishes, as was clearly evident from the numerous empty glasses perched precariously on the kitchen dresser and strewn around from the scullery table to the windowsills outside.

A warm summer night in June provided ideal conditions for the men to 'cool off' and stay close to the half barrel mounted on a wooden box outside the back door, whilst indoors the village women were busy dispensing mugs of strong tea accompanied by a slice of seed loaf liberally spread with strawberry jam.

In her young days, Sarah had crocheted a magnificent white quilt which few people had the opportunity to admire. Somewhat ruffled she explicitly instructed her daughter, Alice, to place the quilt beneath her when she was laid out on her bed, insisting that if people hadn't complimented her on her great work when she was alive, they would most assuredly do so when she was dead.

Billy's thoughts had wandered as the last prayers were said. Most of the crowd had moved away towards the village but he didn't intend to join the funeral party. He was not a man for the pub. At thirty two, this very attractive dark haired, six-foot-one hunk was practically a social outcast of his own making, and referred to locally as a confirmed bachelor. On Sunday nights when the lads of the village were sleeking their hair with Brilliantine in preparation for the all night dances, Billy was content to remain at home leafing through 'Dublin Opinion'.

He was not a man for the girls he told himself. He never had a girlfriend. Never thought about marriage ... well perhaps he did in a peripheral sort of way but with two women, his mother and his grandmother in the house already, who needed a third?

Maintaining self restraint was an endurance test already stretched to its limits but Billy realised that those two ladies had no perception of their own domineering temperaments.

He worked extremely hard on their thirty acre farm, but never quite managed to reach the high standards expected from the women in his life.

Billy became aware of his surroundings when his mother returned to find him still standing beside his grandmother's grave.

"Go down and get your father out of that pub before he makes a show of us," she ordered testily, adding, "Your grandmother is not here to defend him now. He'll hear about this."

He would indeed. Old Sarah always supported her son-in-law stoutly and John Murphy assured himself of her valiant back-up by pressing a Baby Power into her gnarled hands each time he got 'delayed' in town. Sarah effectively reduced everyone to silence after two or three swigs from the bottle.

Sarah also championed her grandson on the many occasions when his single status was criticised by his mother. Grandma placated her daughter with her invariable words of wisdom,

"Leave him be Alice. He'll make a good match when the time is right. You mark my words."

Billy had grave misgivings about that and this 'good match' bit ...well he'd do his own matchmaking, thank you very much. That wily old bird probably had a list of 'suitable matches' tucked underneath her feather mattress.

Now Ma was nudging him towards the pub on an errand he was loathe to undertake. He'd never done this before and felt gauche and ill at ease as he contemplated the look his father would cast in his direction.

"Come on," he mouthed urgently when he finally managed to catch his eye but that intoxicated man simply shook his head indicating three frothy pints of Guinness in front of him.

"When I sink these, son," he managed to splutter at last.

After six hours of reasonably steady drinking, John was plagued by the uncertainty as to whether they were celebrating or commiserating, but sure what the ... he'd give them a verse of *'The Rocks of Bawn'* anyway. It always went down well with a few jars.

Billy's embarrassment was acute. He raised his father to a standing position and moved him to the exit with an admirable display of self control, pausing for an instant to wipe the sweat from his overheated brow once he was outside the door. They walked home in silence and Billy wished with all his heart that grandma was there to act as a buffer when his parents confronted each other. He fled to the fields and let his father take a well earned ear-bashing for once.

After the funeral they settled down to life without grandma at the farm, missing her more than they thought possible. Hay-making time was fast approaching and help was desperately needed with the work. John Murphy spent very little time farming as the days went by. Billy could understand his reasons, as the farm was passed down from his grandmother to his mother, and subsequently to Billy, which peeved the older man considerably and sowed the seeds of apathy.

Grandma had been very decisive. She was genuinely fond of her son-in-law, but believed implicitly that he 'hadn't the makin's' of a good farmer.

For a full week Billy toyed with the idea of advertising for a helper before suggesting it to his parents.

"Surely we can manage ten shillings a week, all found," he ventured tentatively and surprisingly they agreed.

"Wanted. Young person as farm helper. Live in. Some knowledge would suit."

This ad brought some results and Ma took it upon herself to pore over each reply, proclaiming that she was 'a fair good judge of personality' and 'could describe a person accurately from their hand-writing'.

"Now ... this boy, Paddie Molloy, sounds just about right for us," she declared as she opened the fourth envelope. "He seems neat and tidy even if his spelling is hopeless ... and having worked on various farms he would welcome a change."

Her eyebrow shot up in a question mark as she glanced over her glasses at Billy who nodded his head meekly. Two weeks and three letters later, Paddie Molloy was expected to arrive at the farm much to Billy's relief.

"Plucky little youngster," Ma said as she busied herself removing all the unwanted clutter from grandma's bedroom. "He's making his own way from Limerick," she added, "and bringing his bike on the train."

"I have a notion to put the small brass bed in the corner of your room," she suggested lightly to Billy. "That way I could keep grandma's room free in case Aunt Nora decides to visit."

"Not a hope, Ma," he cut in cheerfully but firmly. "The small bed stays here," he insisted as he helped her with the blankets.

He was to recall this weeks later with much amusement and visualise Ma's ticklish situation if she had indeed forged ahead with her great notion.

They had practically given up hope of seeing 'young Molloy' that evening when a tweed jacketed cyclist came pedalling energetically along the boreen towards the house. Billy strode leisurely to greet the navy-trousered newcomer who was dismounting and lifting a suitcase from the carrier of the bike. He watched in astonishment as a red woolly cap was removed to reveal beautiful cascading soft brown hair. Then the owner, with the most angelic blue eyes, extended her hand and said breezily.

"I'm Paddie Molloy ...... it took me quite a while to find this place."

Billy's heart jolted. Ma made many mistakes but this was the most beautiful one ever. Words failed him completely while he stared in fascination at the slim five foot-five young lady as she withdrew her cycle clips from her trousers and patted an unusually welcoming Chester at the same time.

"Come and meet my parents," was all Billy could manage to say, dreading the inevitable scene that would follow.

"Saints in Heaven preserve us," Ma exclaimed loudly, totally unable to grasp the situation.

"Has your brother changed his mind?" she asked sharply, hoping the girl had just come to make excuses for him.

No such luck. Paddie Molloy spent the next ten minutes explaining her real name was Patricia, but she was known to everyone as Paddie all her life. Apologising profusely for the confusion, she told them of her great ambition to have her own farm one day, and was moving around to gain all the farming experience available to her in the meantime. Noting the scepticism on the older woman's face, Paddie deftly moved in to acquaint them with her frustration on arriving at the local station, to find she must cycle a further six miles before she reached her destination.

"Billy would have met you if we had known," Mrs Murphy told her, secure in the belief that her son would have dispatched that young woman back to Limerick on the next train.

Not so. Once the initial shock wore off, Billy actually relished the idea of having female company, especially one so attractive. She looked more beautiful each day he decided, and not just that ...... she could turn her hand to everything. They worked together in perfect unison, and the former silent and withdrawn Billy was transformed into a smiling, happy man. Paddie Molloy was certainly doing strange things to his irregularly beating heart.

"He's going around like a love-sick school-boy," Ma announced with a knowing wink, scenting an early romance which her husband failed to see.

She eagerly awaited some nice news as the weeks fled by. Paddie had wormed her way into all their hearts, she realised, helping indoors at every available opportunity, and that once dubious woman was melting visibly with such unaccustomed cosseting.

"I thought you'd never ask me," a jubilant Paddie replied when Billy finally asked her to marry him.

Three months later as they left for the church on their wedding day, Billy paused for a moment to look at the large photograph on the mantlepiece.

"You old schemer, Grandma," he whispered fondly as if she could hear him. "You were right all the time. We're a good match and the timing is …… perfect."

# Anne Morrin

*The most reliable transport of all*

CHAPTER 15

# Autumnal Reflections

K ATE'S EYES POPPED OPEN as the sound of Pat's voice disturbed the peace and quiet of the early autumn morning.

"C'mon Kate," he pleaded urgently, his eyes fastened on the grandfather clock in the corner of the room.

"Dowd'll be here at nine and we still have to clean out the barn," he reminded her, tugging at the blankets while Kate held them firmly beneath her chin.

Her eyes followed his. It wasn't even six o'clock yet, for heavens sake. Obviously it was going to be 'one of these days'. The thrasher was coming and Pat was anxious and impatient to start preparations for a busy day ahead.

Kate knew perfectly well who would clean out the barn, like last year and all the other years, when Reilly's barn had to accommodate all the bags of grain as they were unhooked from the thrasher, and carried to safety immediately 'in case it rained'. She also knew it was going to be an extremely busy day for her, providing meals for the gang, mostly neighbours, who gathered together to 'give a hand', as the thrasher moved from one haggard to the next throughout the village.

Kate fervently hoped Pat would not take on that backbreaking task of hauling the grain indoors. She was sick of 'risin' bags' on his back. He could not manage without her assistance, and a day of hoisting heavy grain bags left her with aching limbs for hours. She wished he would leave the donkey-work to the younger men, but Pat reckoned he was more than a match for any young fella.

"Why shouldn't he, when I'm the one who does all the liftin'," she thought crossly as she headed for the barn with her brush and shovel.

Kate was a petite fair-haired young woman of twenty-five, with a very attractive face, while her husband Pat was a long, lean, dark-haired man of forty-six, with strongly hewn features, conveying the impression of constantly battling with the elements. Despite the fact that he had no more than a tiny sprinkling of grey at his temples, he looked much older than his years.

Family and friends expressed concern at such an impracticable union with a man old enough to be her father. Her parents in particular hoped their shy retiring daughter would abandon her self-imposed seclusion and head for Dublin's bright lights with her sisters. Instead she married Pat Reilly at nineteen, and settled in the little thatched cottage with tea-roses rambling round the door, and red geraniums flowering profusely in any discarded old bucket she could find.

Few eyebrows would have been raised even in those far off days of the thirties and forties, if she had packed her bags and left. She was totally unsuitable as a farmer's wife, some said, but for 'a little slip of a thing' she surprised them all by working extremely hard, forever anxious to please her spouse. Pat was a stubborn man set in his ways, and Kate's 'new-fangled' suggestions for reducing the work-load on their scattered little farm were very hastily dismissed.

"Good oul'-fashioned hard labour never hurt anyone," he remarked with casual indifference.

At such times she wondered if her uncle, who had brought them together, had been a bit lavish in his praise of this generous, placid, kind-hearted man, and instantly regretted such undeserving disloyalty. Her heart told her Pat was one of the best. She gathered up her brush and shovel and went indoors to prepare a 'snack' for the workmen.

Mick Dowd always arrived on time for thrashing, but his tractor, becoming more erratic with age, took longer than usual to coax into action. There was no time for breakfast, but what better place to be going to than Reillys? Kate would be out with tea and brown bread for the gang before work commenced in the haggard.

"Why the heck did she marry so young?" he asked himself as he sprinted with admirable agility onto the tractor seat, and drove along the narrow boreen.

He rarely indulged in such thoughts. Probably an autumnal phase re-kindled annually when he met her on thrashing-day, he decided. Memories of other days crept into his mind reluctantly, of their eighteen months romance when both were very young and happy as sandboys. He remembered her adoration and puppy-love, and his rash assumption that she was 'tying him down'. He fled from the neighbourhood without a word, with total disregard for her feelings.

She was married and beyond reach when he returned, which was just as well, perhaps. He could never hope to re-gain her trust after his impulsive and cowardly action. Only he knew how bitterly he regretted his impetuous conduct. Lots of girls had come and gone in his life since then, but as yet, at twenty-eight, he had no particular desire to marry. A confirmed bachelor, he presumed lightly, pushing thoughts of Kate from his mind as he drove into Pat Reilly's haggard.

Thrashing commenced when morning tea was over, and very soon Pat was urging his wife to get the grain indoors ...... although the sky was cloudless. After two hours of 'risin' bags' on his back she was scurrying to the kitchen to prepare dinner. Huge quantities of bacon and cabbage and potatoes had to be cooked to satisfy their enormous appetites. It was comforting to know that catering for twelve hungry farmers was not an everyday chore, she thought dryly, placing a mountain of food in front of each man at the table.

"Thank Goodness that's over," Kate spoke aloud while she stacked the washed plates on the dresser. She leaned against it with the tea-towel slung over her shoulder and allowed memories of Mick Dowd and their young love to overflow. He was her whole world then, so tall, so handsome, with his brown wavy hair always mussed from absently raking his fingers through it. She had literally thrown herself at him and cringed with shame afterwards. She smiled wistfully now. In hindsight she did nothing more than hold him tightly in her arms and whisper, "I'll love you forever", but obviously it was enough to send him running scared.

For a moment she re-lived the days and nights of torment, battling with unrequited love. She was young and innocent then, and it had hurt unbearably, she remembered, as steady, dependable Pat hurried into the kitchen shattering her reverie.

"Make a few apple-tarts for the tay," he suggested, "an' a few curran' buns while ye'r at it. That's my girl."

She shrugged resignedly. Her husband always insisted on a mid-afternoon tea-break for the gang. They worked better on full stomachs.

Gazing idly around the haggard while they ate, Kate reflected on the upswing in thrashing techniques in recent years. Prior to this, the farmers had no option but to 'flail' or 'slash' the sheaves of corn to remove the grain. It was long and laborious work. No one regretted its passing, she mused, gathering up the empty mugs and basket.

Except for the occasional barking of a dog, a hushed silence fell over the entire village when Mick Dowd finally switched off his tractor as darkness crept stealthily over the haggard. Once again the men traipsed into the kitchen to partake of a late evening supper. They lingered on, discussing various aspects of farming while Kate replenished their mugs for the third time. Eventually they bade their goodnights and strolled to their respective homes at midnight.

Kate was weary in mind and body. She looked with distaste at the unwashed crockery on the table. Let it wait, she decided. Kicking off her shoes she eased her aching limbs into the old rocking chair in the corner, and thought about tomorrow and cleaning up the haggard which now resembled a ploughed field. Despite her best efforts her eyelids fluttered and then closed tightly. Silence descended on the kitchen like a thickening fog.

From a great distance she could hear Pat calling. Her eyes refused to open but she knew he was there, absently raking his fingers through his wavy brown hair and giving her that gorgeous smile that always brought a lovely warm glow to her heart. All of which was very confusing, as Pat had straight hair and his smile was like the man himself..... sincere, steadfast, and intensely loyal.

# Anne Morrin

*A busy day on the farm*

CHAPTER 16

# Farewell To Connemara

*'For to see again the moonlight over Claddagh,
An' watch the sun go down o'er Galway Bay'*

JAMSIE'S HEART SANG HAPPILY. He was vaguely aware of the sound of rushing water and snuggled down contentedly beneath the threadbare blankets on the hard unyielding iron bed. Ye couldn't bate it, he thought, floating off to dreamland. It must be the loveliest sound in the whole world. The sound of the waves pounding on the shore near Leiter Calaidh. He tried to sing at full volume, but failed to get the words out, and then his brother, Peader, was shaking him roughly, throwing the blankets on to the floor at the same time, and yelling,

"A'ye goin' to get up at all to-day, ye lazy eejit?"

Somewhat disorientated, he sprang out of bed and pelted to the small cobweb-covered window, expecting to see the Atlantic before his eyes, but there was nothing except the familiar sight of other peoples back-yards …….so tiny and so full of rubbish. Tears blurred his eyes. There was no sea. No Leitir Calaidh. No pounding waves on the shore. Just Peader, slashin' cold water into the tin basin to wash his face, an' makin' enough of a racket to wake the dead.

Jamsie sat on the edge of the bed and fought back the tears. Tears for everything he longed for……Connemara, the sea, the wide open spaces, and the freedom. He hated it here in Camden Town, with their "Ye can't do this an' ye can't do that" all day and every day. There wasn't wan to say "How'ya Jamsie. How's it goin'?" when he went down to the corner shop for a loaf. The loneliness was unbearable at times.

Jamsie shared a tiny bedroom with Peader where they ate, slept and washed. That was in the spring of 1949 when Jamsie was eighteen and Peader thought it was time he stopped scroungin' off th' oul' pair at home an' earned his own livin'. Jamsie actually looked forward to it all until he realised that this cramped little space was going to be his home for the foreseeable future.

Their little thatched cottage at home in Connemara was small….very small….but it was vast when compared to the bloody biscuit-tin they were packed into now, he sobbed angrily.

"Ye'll do fine," Peader assured him airily when he was home for Christmas.

"I'll getcha a job. All ye have to do is get off yer lazy butt an' work….just like everyone else."

He was right of course. All the lads he went to school with were leaving one by one for the big cities in England. Some of them didn't come home very often, but most of them DID turn up when their oul' fellas or oul' ladies died, an' they were always wearin' brand new black suits, an' a spankin' white shirt with the collar out over the jacket.

"That's the first thing every lad saves up for," Peader confided in deadly earnestness.

"The black suit is a 'must' in case ye have to go home in a hurry. It's nice for Mass and the pub on Sundays as well. Ye feel as good as everyone else."

"An' they manage to have a few bob in their pockets too," Peader continued, warming to his subject. Its great to be able to buy yer round like a true Connemara man......when the time comes," he added meaningly.

It sounded all right, but Jamsie refused to dwell on the black suit for long. It gave him the creeps to even think of such a thing. He swung himself off the edge of the bed and swore he'd go home that evening, but common sense prevailed in a moment. He hadn't enough money to bring him to Euston station, much less to go home. Pay-day was still three days away.

Th'oul' couple at home were in fine fettle, he assured himself. Sure th'oul' fella gave in to Peader the Christmas before last and went over to Camden Town to see the sights for himself. He took one look at the block o' flats and said,

"God, ye have a fierce big house, Peter. Is there much land in wit' it?"

Trying hard not to laugh, Peader pointed to the window box containing a little sprig of Connemara heather, on the 5th floor where he lived, and quipped,

"They don't have big farms around here. Just enough to rear a few maggots."

Th' oul' fella had *'no meas'* on Camden Town after that. There wasn't a cabbage-patch to be seen, an' not a sight of the 'sae' anywhere, he thought moodily, longing for the sound of the waves crashing against the rocks when the oft-times unpredictable ocean got its dander up. He was convinced he would suffocate if he stayed much longer, and the day Peader packed him off home with Mrs. McDonagh from Leitir Moir, who was goin' over to see her mother, he knew he would never see Camden Town or any other part of London ever again.

"Ye can take the man outta the bog, but ye can't take the bog outta the man," Jamsie remembered, kicking the worn raffia mat across the floor, and anyway, how could th' oul' fella be expected to adjust when he himself was findin' it tough goin', he thought forlornly.

It seemed so manly when he was at home to refer to his parents as th' oul' couple, just like everyone else did, but suddenly he realised they were far from old.

The oul' fella was fifty-seven but he acted like he was a hundred and fifty-seven. His mother was fifty-one, but seemed much older. No wonder they called her th' oul' lady, he thought indulgently, remembering the times when Peader or Johnnie came home from England. She had the knife sharpened and was off to the hen-house to behead one of the cocks. The lads were sure of boiled chicken and soup within a couple of hours of their arrival.

Th' oul' lady was a familiar sight, sauntering along by the gable-end of the house, holding the dead bird by the legs, head downwards, to ensure all its blood had drained away before she removed its feathers and innards, prior to cooking. Jamsie could see her now with little rivulets of blood skidding down her apron, to settle on her heavy well-worn shoes, and could almost hear her ordering him to get the spade an' dig a few stalks o' spuds before the lads arrived.

It was the same every year. Jamsie felt it was a bit like the return of the prodigal son with the amount of fuss th' oul' lady was makin'. Chicken to-day; home-cured fat bacon and cabbage to-morrow; fresh fish the day after. She fed them like pigs, Jamsie knew only too well, an' they took it all for granted. Never a thought for all the brown bread she was baking, or the fact that th' oul' fella was grumblin' about goin' aisy on the turf when he'd see so much extra being used for cookin'.

Well......wan thing for sure, Jamsie told himself stoutly, she wouldn't be workin' her fingers to the bone whenever

## The Ireland We Remember

HE went back home. There would be none of those stomach-bulging dinners for him. Not that he didn't love them...... he did. But he had a sudden compelling desire to treat his mother like a lady. He'd do all the cooking himself, and he'd never refer to her as th' oul' lady again. She deserved better than that. He wiped his eyes with the back of his hand, and in a moment of defiance he almost decided to ignore Peaders oul' talk about the black suit, and save up for a nice costume for his mother instead.

Peader was yelling again,

"We're going to the Galtymore in Cricklewood to-night with the lads. It'll be great *craic*. Plenty o'wimmen an' lots o' booze. An' don't forget it's your turn to boil the dinner this evening," he reminded him, banging the door behind him.

Jamsie didn't really want to go. Although he was tall, fair-haired and good-looking, he was, at best, rather shy, and generally avoided crowds. Still, it was better than lying awake all night listening to that awful racket overhead. Those people seemed to come alive around midnight.

The communal gas cooker was at one end of the corridor, and here tenants had to await their turn to cook dinner after work, as most rooms were not, as yet, equipped with cooking facilities.

Mornings at the other end of the corridor where the communal toilet was situated presented a more serious problem with everyone rushing and queuing for their turn. Long delays resulted in Mother Nature getting all the blame for the damp patches on the faded, well-worn tarpaulin.

Jamsie detested the cramped conditions he lived in, and fervently hoped that one day he would have his very own accommodation. Self-contained flats were the coming thing. Suddenly he felt much better and decided to join the lads for this great night out.

They enjoyed themselves immensely. Jamsie couldn't be shy for long with such a nice crowd. The music tugged at his heart-strings until the urge to dance became irresistible. Having convinced himself beforehand that he would be refused, it was like heady wine when the girls gladly accepted his invitation to dance with him. His self-confidence soared. He felt so manly, having his first sweet taste of 'being in demand'.

It was long after midnight when he saw her. Like an apparition, he thought in silent wonder. Nowhere in the world could there be a more beautiful vision. Men were crowding around, asking her to dance, but her eyes were on Jamsie, with the most adorable come-hither look.

Totally out of character, he grabbed her quickly, almost catapulting her on to the dance-floor, where they fell around in helpless laughter. They danced together in perfect unison, and the fact that Noreen McDonagh hailed from nearby *Tir An Fhia* in Connemara did much to cement the beginnings of a lovely new relationship. They had so much in common. So much to talk about. Jamsie wished the night would go on forever. Later, when the band played…

> 'For to see again the moonlight over Claddagh,
> An' watch the sun go down o'er Galway Bay'

…it was almost as if it was played specially for them. Jamsie would never, ever, forget that night in The Galtymore when he first met the girl who later became Mrs. Jamsie Flaherty.

## The Ireland We Remember

*'The sea, oh the sea'*

CHAPTER 17

# Spellbound

KATE SULLIVAN STUDIED HER father's face as he hurried down the hill from Camillaun House. His jaunty step and the brief 'thumbs-up' sign he gave her as he passed the kitchen window was an indication that something exciting was afoot up at the Big House. Pushing his cap off his sweaty brow he blurted out,

"Master Alan wants to speak to ye immediately........ about teachin' the kids, no less," he added importantly.

Kate stared at him for a second, then feigning indifference, said off-handedly,

"Is that all," and resumed the washing-up.

"He's goin' to offer ye a job," Tom Sullivan pointed out with barely concealed impatience, noting the mutinous expression slipping into place, and the negative shake of her head.

"I thought ye'd be glad o' the chance," he exclaimed in disbelief, wiping his brow frustratedly with his mucky cap.

"Teachin' kids is what'ye do best," he reasoned, "can ye not even talk to the man? He wants a governess an' you want the work."

Kate interrupted him rudely,

"Who told him that? You of course," she stormed, banging saucepans into the sink with unnecessary force. "You discussed ME with that self-opinionated bighead," she exploded heatedly. "Well, I'll thank you to mind your own business. I'm perfectly capable of finding my own employment."

"Have ye got something against the man?" her father demanded, his face flushing a dull angry red. "Ya haven't seen him in years. He's good enough to give ye first refusal, but it seems there's no pleasin' some wimmen," he added, as he strode out, banging the door loudly behind him.

Kate realised he was both angry and disappointed, and instantly regretted her callous outburst. She knew how deeply upset he was when she lost her job at the local school owing to a dramatic decrease in child numbers. Opening the door hastily she called after him,

"Just give me a little time to think about it ......... please."

He nodded dejectedly, shoulders drooping, and ambled to the tool-shed to cool down. How could anyone refuse to work in such a magnificent mansion, he wondered?

Camillaun House was, in the carefully chosen words of the old squire, its former owner, 'a suave aristocrat among noble abodes', with its windswept and aged stone façade, and its outstanding Gothic battlements. An 18th century millionaire's home with its imposing three floors over the basement, and all its period features still intact. Soft velvety green lawns meandered down to Lough Corrib shore from the terrace above, while privacy from the road was protected by huge poplars and dense shrubbery.

The rear boasted a cobbled courtyard, six loose boxes with extensive lofting, and a cut-stone two-bedroom cottage for the gardener, where the kitchen window looked towards the Big House, standing among the trees on the hill, like a silent sentinel.

Although Kate lived in the cottage with her parents for most of her young life, she knew Alan Baxter, the old squire's son, only slightly. She well remembered as teenagers, if they met unexpectedly on the avenue, he swept off his silly cap with exaggerated politeness, bending forward but never speaking.

"Cat got yer tongue," she'd hiss, just loud enough for him to hear.

Such haughty and arrogant behaviour provoked vicious yearnings to turn around swiftly and deliver a resounding kick up behind, thereby rooting his aristocratic nose in the rough gravel beneath their feet. She managed to resist such impulses, as reckless, unladylike conduct would never be tolerated by her parents who obviously idolized that overbearing stuffed shirt. Tom Sullivan made himself crystal clear when his then sixteen-year old daughter flared up about Master Alan's boorishness.

"Yer only huffed because he doesn't make a fuss o'ye," he teased at first, in an effort to lighten her mood, but eventually silenced further outbursts with a sharp rebuke,

"Now, now, young lady, no name-callin'. Stop slammin' the lad. Not another word outta ye. He'll make a fine man one day, ye'll see."

An uncomfortable thought persisted now, that her father was correct. She HAD wanted Master Alan to notice her and make a fuss of her. Did her father also guess that she made special efforts to waylay him until he spurned her rudely? Her face burned with humiliation at the thought.

The realization as she grew older, that the squire's son was not allowed to mix with local youngsters did little towards conciliation. Kate was of the unshakable opinion that the desired object was to lord it over them all. All of which contributed to her assumption that Master Alan was an insolent strutting peacock, but how she wished her father would dispense with that juvenile mode of address demanded from the staff by the boy's mother, that flighty lady who abandoned her child and her home for the bright lights of London.

Master Alan saw little of his father, and regarded Tom Sullivan as a father figure and confidant. In later years when his young wife was thrown from her horse and killed, it was to Tom he turned for comfort.

Contrary to her feigned lack of interest earlier, Kate was astonished that Alan Baxter even remembered her. Their paths had not crossed for eight years. She was twenty-four now and the 'Baxter boy' must be twenty-nine. She had no clear concept of what he looked like, and it was quite possible he would not recognise her either if they met beyond the confines of the Big House.

Stifling her stubborn pride, she had completed her toilette for her interview when her father's voice broke into her thoughts,

"I'm glad ye changed yer mind. He won't bite," he said gruffly, his anger having abated somewhat.

With a sceptical look she swept out the back door and walked up the hill, holding her head high.

The massive oak door was opened immediately by Edith, the elderly housekeeper, who ushered Kate into the study where Alan Baxter obviously awaited her arrival.

"Miss Sullivan, Sir," Edith announced, as he came forward with extended hand.

"Thank you for coming, Miss Sullivan," he said, shaking her hand absently. "I shall not detain you long."

His eyes followed her in an abstract fashion as she seated herself in the chair he had indicated. Then as if shaking off something intangible, some insubstantial thing, he sat behind the big mahogany desk and said formally,

"Let's begin, shall we?"

Kate almost gasped aloud. She fervently hoped he did not notice her open mouth and popping eyes. Alan Baxter certainly had changed. The lanky pimple-faced youth of yesteryear was replaced by a well-fleshed, devastatingly attractive man. Cold, remote and infuriatingly haughty-looking as ever, but divinely handsome nonetheless.

The normally unflappable young woman in the male arena was now somewhat discomfited to find her pulse-rate escalating rapidly. She expected matureness, but was totally unprepared for this magnificent hunk sitting opposite her.

Opening her briefcase, she slid some papers across the desk in his direction.

"My references, Mr. Baxter. I think you will find I am a competent teacher," she said stiffly.

"I already know that," he replied brusquely, returning her papers after a cursory glance at the contents, then leaning forward he gazed at her momentarily with his wonderful magnetic eyes, sending the adrenalin coursing through her veins.

"I also know you are Tom's daughter, and that in itself is adequate recommendation for me," he said slowly, hypnotizing her for evermore with a penetrating blue stare.

She was completely flustered and ill at ease. Vainly, she tried to still her beating heart and command her mind to return to the business on hand, whilst Alan Baxter startled her by saying,

"I would be deeply honoured if you would accept the position," and Kate startled herself much more with an affirmative nod of her head and a decidedly jittery,

"Thank you."

He responded instantly with one of those potentially bone-melting smiles that did strange things to her cold, unforgiving heart. It would be lunacy to work for such an utterly fascinating man, she conceded, but heady, intoxicating lunacy nevertheless. Love him or loathe him, no female could resist him - except Kate Sullivan, she thought defiantly.

Up at the Big House Alan Baxter still sat behind his desk and told himself it was absolute folly to employ Tom's daughter. She was a stunningly beautiful girl, and a sixth sense warned him that she could well and truly shatter his peace of mind. However, it was a thrilling prospect.......... She was utterly bewitching. Gone forever was the tomboy freckly youngster he remembered. The woman she had become was exquisite, well groomed and graceful.

He knew she was remembering also, and could see the scorn in her eyes throughout their brief interview. He had difficulty maintaining his haughty image when his heartbeats were quickening like a lovesick teenager. Exceptionally rare sensations invaded his being, and concentration on everyday tasks became impossible. His thoughts were entirely on an exciting tomorrow when that dazzling, disdainful, damsel would commence work at Camillaun House.

*He could feel her dislike throughout their brief interview*

CHAPTER 18

# Behind Closed Doors

KATE SULLIVAN CROSSED THE terrace and climbed the steps nimbly to the huge oak door of Camillaun House. She wondered, not for the first time that morning, what sort of madness possessed her the previous day when she accepted the offer of a job from that arrogant blue-blood, Alan Baxter.

Accepting ANYTHING from Mr. STRUTTING PEACOCK was 'the last stone in her beads' she told herself haughtily, while she waited for Edith, the elderly housekeeper to open the door. She refused to dwell on the unpalatable truth that she was so completely bowled over by the magnificent hunk who did strange things to her heart, that she said "Thank you" like an excited school-girl.

"Miss Sullivan, Sir," Edith announced formally, while Kate stepped into the large study which seemed dark and unfriendly on that first day.

Alan Baxter greeted her with a courteous "good morning" and began, "I am deeply indebted to you for accepting my offer," while Kate thought sceptically,

"Spare me the humbug and get on with it."

"You are a school teacher," he continued, "with all the essential qualifications to educate and discipline my," ….. here he smiled faintly and quirked one eyebrow ….. "my slightly unruly children. I shall leave them in your very capable hands. You will find everything you need in the school-room."

Then, as if anxious to be rid of her, he walked across the study and held open the door. Instantly, two pretty little girls scampered across the corridor and vanished into the drawing-room. They had been taking turns at peeping through the keyhole to get a glimpse of the new governess, they admitted later that day.

Wearing his 'no nonsense' face, Alan Baxter strode purposefully towards the drawing-room door, while unconsciously, Kate reached out a restraining hand, saying impulsively,

"Were you never a mischievous child yourself, Mr. Baxter?"

She regretted her impetuous action immediately, when he stopped and silenced her with a cold bleak look. For one heart-stopping second she thought "I've blown it", and began to apologise, but he interrupted her with a stiff,

"You are quite right, of course …. Katie ….. Miss Sullivan," and retraced his steps.

What on earth got into him to make a slip-up like that? He hoped, rather shame-facedly, that she hadn't heard, but Kate thought her name never sounded so smooth, so velvety, so silky ever before, on anyone's lips.

He stood beside her lost in thought, but Kate was not to know her words had jogged painful memories of the little boy who wistfully longed to misbehave like other little boys.

The same boy who looked down from his bedroom window, lonely and close to tears, while he watched the village children playing in the fields, long after he himself, was sent to his bed. He never dared to put a foot wrong, and there were times when he envied Kate, he recalled now. Her parents, Tom and Anne-Marie, were so flexible, allowing her to wander about at will with the workmen and their families, whilst he must remain aloof at all times.

Kate's father, Tom, and Edith, the housekeeper, were the only staff members he was allowed to talk to. Good, motherly, big-hearted Edith who loved him, cuddled him, and fed him as if he were her very own. He had four governesses in quick succession but they remained cold and remote always, and the day he was sent to boarding school at the tender age of twelve, and Tom and Edith were stuffing him into his navy-nap coat and cap, he failed dismally to blink back the lonely tears.

Kate despised him then, as she did now. It was written all over her stunningly beautiful face. Their young days kept creeping back most uncomfortably. Like an insect crawling along the skin, he thought. A part of you wanted to flick it off and forget it, while another part of you wanted to hold it and watch its progress with rapt attention.

He could vividly recall her adoration and puppy love of their teenage years, and not without shame, his own brash, uncouth reaction. He had gone to college soon afterwards, but not before he had seen the hurt and scorn in her eyes. Her unhappy little face haunted his dreams for months.

When he returned to Camillaun House for Christmas holidays, Tom told him, conversationally, that "my Katie is gone away to train. She's going to be a school-teacher one day."

It was then he whole-heartedly wished he had been spunky enough to disobey strict parental orders and at least acknowledge Kate's presence when they met occasionally on the driveway. Suddenly, as if he just remembered she was still standing beside him, he touched her arm and said brightly,

"Come to the kitchen and talk to Edith. She will show you over the house and introduce you to the children. Right?"

Right. You pompous oul' stuffed shirt. She almost said the words aloud in her anger. Surely it was his duty, as a father, to prepare his children for a new teacher, and at least make the introductions himself? Of all the crass idiots, she fumed silently. Small wonder they were running around peeping through key-holes.

Alan Baxter marched ahead of her to the kitchen to find the housekeeper putting breakfast on the table for the children, which came as a surprise to Kate, who assumed that "big shots" and their families always breakfasted in the morning-room.

"Edith, you have already met Miss Sullivan," he said pleasantly, and turning to Kate, he continued,

"And, you, of course, have already met Mrs. Connors ………Miss Sullivan."

A startled Kate watched uneasily as Edith slapped Alan Baxter playfully with a tea-towel, and said laughingly,

"Get on with you, Alan. It's only little Katie from the cottage. Come in, love, and we'll look after the children first. Then we'll have a nice cuppa tea an' a chat."

Kate smiled inwardly as she pondered on the 'Miss Sullivan, Sir,' on both occasions when Edith announced her. That pair certainly knew how to keep up appearances.

She was startled even more when Edith shooed him towards the door, reminding him he had work to do. He grinned impishly, dipping his finger in the sugar-bowl as he went, and Kate's heart beat rapidly at the sight of a lovable, boyish smile spreading across his absolutely splendid face as he sauntered down the hallway.

"He's having lunch with Colonel and Mrs. Whyte today," Edith offered by way of explanation. "They hope he can spare a few hours to go fishing on the lake …….. and, perhaps land a big trout. But for now, let's find those kids and fill their little bellies. Then we can talk."

What about my work, Kate wondered, but kept silent. Camillaun House was so easy-going behind its closed doors, and Edith was so warm, so motherly, Kate could almost understand Alan Baxter's relaxed mood. Didn't her father always say that himself and Edith practically reared Master Alan between them?

In the months that followed, he visited the school-room every morning to see his little girls, Fern and Rebecca, who were so lovable and a joy to teach. His aloof and haughty manner was fading gradually, and he was constantly alternating between friendship and apparent indifference, but during his moments of witticism, the sun shone in her heart when she saw his face soften and his smile crinkling up the corners of his eyes.

She was becoming completely besotted with this gorgeous hunk of virile manhood. He only had to give her one of his slow smouldering looks to set her heart hammering irregularly, and have her fretting about her hair, her face and her figure. Fortunately for her, she had a face that required very little maintenance, but that never stopped her from sprinting to her mirror for a quick peek when she heard his footsteps in the hallway. She could cope with the hackle-raising arrogance that made prickles stir on the back of her neck, but this new, unexpectedly tender heart-throb was her undoing. Oh God, who is the crass idiot now, she wondered glumly.

As for Alan Baxter, his whole world had changed since Kate commenced work at Camillaun House. She continually disturbed his peace of mind, but such pleasurable disturbance gladdened his heart and put a spring in his step.

## Anne Morrin

The golden girl who occupied his thoughts all day and invaded his dreams at night, brought a ray of sunshine into his home every morning. She had wormed her way into his lonely heart until he could no longer hide his true feelings. He desperately longed to hold her in his arms and smooth away the hurt and misunderstandings of their teenage years. But most of all, he wanted to tell her he loved her, passionately, and forever, knowing deep in his heart that his life would be meaningless without his incredibly beautiful Kate.

# The Ireland We Remember

*Like any mother and son behind closed doors*

CHAPTER 19

# Home Is Where The Heart Is

It was one of those hazy, cobwebby, sunshiny mornings with tiny midges pinching your skin if you stood still for a second. Eileen Duffy waited impatiently for the bus, already ten minutes overdue, which would take her to Galway.

Relieved to be indoors at last from such an army of starving insects, Eileen chose a seat by the window and watched the landscape varying from high rocky mountains still shrouded in mist, to low lying bogland and stretches of uncultivated terrain, peopled only by curlews and gulls.

As the bus laboured painfully up the steep hills and freewheeled down into the barren valleys below, the few 'mountainy' sheep on the roadside raised their heads inquisitively, and then stared in mild annoyance at the noisy dawdling petrol-guzzler which threatened to disturb the serenity and the wild beauty of the early morning in the hinterland of Connemara.

Two months previously a bus service was introduced to the area, bringing infinite joy into the lives of the local people, who could at last travel to Galway city and shop for spades and shovels, buckets and beer, in addition to boots and drapery. All purchases were brought home on the bus. The driver could expect anything. Even the cheeping of day-old chicks from the boxes on the back seats.

As they rocked and rolled their way into Galway, Eileen recalled once again her utter dejection on the day twelve years ago when the parish priest, Father Matthew, walked into the classroom and announced that she would be transferred from her beloved national school in Ross where she had taught for nine years.

Afterwards she had scolded herself for not 'standing up' to Fr. Matthew. Why hadn't she refused to move? But she already knew the answer. Her fate had been decided and she had no choice other than to succumb to authority.

Catherine and Bartle, whose house aptly named *'Cois Abhainn'* she had shared for those nine years, wept openly when the young girl told them of her forthcoming transfer to Connemara. The elderly couple had done a favour for Fr. Matthew by giving 'digs' to Eileen when she first arrived in Mayo, only to become too attached over the years, accepting her as one of their own. While they believed implicitly that Eileen was happy to remain in Ross forever, they never considered the probability that circumstances could, and indeed frequently did, alter from one year to the next.

Privately Fr. Matthew was to some extent disappointed with the course of recent events, having no-one to blame but himself. He had given glowing accounts of Eileen's prowess as a drama teacher to his friend Fr. Tom, recklessly recommending her services.

"If you ever need someone to raise funds for that old school of yours, just remember what she did for Ross," he confided with great gusto.

Not for a moment did he envisage such a possibility, but Fr. Tom filed it away in his memory. Some months later the wheels of officialdom were put in motion resulting in Eileen's transfer to Connemara some sixty miles away.

Through her unstinting efforts and boundless co-operation from the children, Eileen organised two school concerts each year at Ross, thereby raising sufficient funds to reconstruct the one hundred years old decrepit school, and purchase a new harmonium which was her own particular pride and joy. She had put together a church choir and on Friday evenings four of the senior boys had the unenviable task of transporting her precious harmonium to the local church for Sunday morning Mass.

"That old school in Connemara is in dreadful condition," Fr. Matthew had told Eileen, rubbing the inside of his thumb over his uneven yellow teeth. "Sure you'll be in your element organising a few concerts for Fr. Tom… won't you?" he persisted noting the trembling of her lower lip which suggested she was perilously close to tears.

"You will be as successful in Connemara as you are here," he added soothingly "and the day Fr. Tom's school is rebuilt I'll have you back again in Ross." Then reverting to his old assertive manner he said hurriedly "Now, won't that do you?" as if that were the end of the matter, when in actual fact he was unhappy to be losing one of his best teachers.

Sadly in the intervening years Fr. Matthew passed away and hopes of returning to her adopted village were abandoned forever, despite numerous efforts on Eileen's part to be reinstated. She had been taken away from her school. She knew no world beyond the village of Ross. The transition was extreme. Public transport was practically non-existent for years, and the recent advent of a bus service from Connemara to Galway was a shock of delight for Eileen.

Subsequently, an extended service of a late afternoon bus from Galway to Mayo which actually had a scheduled stop at Ross, fuelled her obsession to return at last. Just to see the familiar faces and places once again. At the first opportunity she was on her way, adrenaline coursing through her body with each passing mile.

Eileen sprang from the bus looking around her with eager expectation. Ross was as beautiful as she remembered it, with the old school standing in isolated splendour on the hill. She strolled past the post office and glanced inside. It was unlikely that the post master would recognise her now, she thought, but surprisingly as she approached the counter he peered over the top of his specs and exclaimed with obvious pleasure,

"Well, well, well, if it isn't young Miss Duffy. Lave it there," proffering his bony hand to shake hers until her teeth almost rattled. "Yeh didn't grow an inch. Still as small as ever," he announced with his usual veracity when he had given her the once-over. "Now," he suggested briskly, indicating the counter-top as a seat, "hop up there and tell me all yer news while I get the post-bag ready for the mail-car."

Eileen had no objections to being considered 'young' and 'small'. She was a bit of both. She measured five-feet-three-inches in her stockings and was the proud possessor of a body as slim and lithe as any youngster. Soft wavy brown hair was swept back from her forehead and held in place with a hair-band to match her outfit for the day. This blue-eyed bespectacled lady was now forty-five and still single, but somehow managed to look ten years younger than her actual years.

She smiled at the 'Miss Duffy'. It was deemed presumptuous in those days to address a teacher by their christian name, an irksome practice which Eileen had learned to accept as she grew older. Eager to explore the village before dusk, she hurriedly took her leave of the postmaster and walked to the bridge to gaze longingly across the river at *'Cois Abhainn'* where she had lived for nine years.

Overcome with curiosity she sauntered along the water's edge and crossed the old foot-bridge to the house. Countless times in the past she had run across that same wooden structure, pausing momentarily in the early summer mornings to watch the velvety flowing movement of the waters below, and the angry churning surge in winter when the river swelled and spilled over the footbridge.

Catherine and Bartle had long since gone to their eternal reward, but whoever owned the place now had no real affection for it, she reflected sadly. It looked cold and bleak stripped naked of its beautiful evergreen ivy, and scantily clad instead in a thin layer of faded cream-coloured paint. But enshrined in Eileen's memory were the rockets and the roses of yester-year, and the box hedge trimmed annually by one of the boys from the school.

Suddenly she realised the house was uninhabited. Outside was neglected and overgrown, and a cursory glance as she passed the windows revealed a conspicuous emptiness, except for the Sacred Heart picture hanging drunkenly on the wall over the kitchen table. Wallowing in nostalgia and somewhat despondent, she was about to retrace her footsteps when she became vaguely conscious of a 'For Sale' sign, green from exposure and dampness, partly hidden behind the unkempt box hedge. Instantly her mind went into overdrive as she struggled with emotions of astonishment and joy. Would that this be true, she prayed silently, savouring the host of possibilities emerging from this discovery.

Her head was overflowing with improbable ideas when she eventually closed the wooden gate behind her and walked round to the village grocery store, expecting to find changes there also. Old Mike the shopkeeper, was sitting on the tea chest reading his newspaper, his only solace he always maintained. She startled him by creeping up behind him, placing her hands over his eyes and playing 'Guess Who'.

At an appropriate moment during their conversation she cautiously broached the subject of *'Cois Abhainn'*, not wishing to appear overly enthusiastic.

"Ah, that's for sale this two years," he told her in his own dismissive way.

"The Yank who bought it reckoned it was too near the river ... it made his asthma worse. He'd sell it chape to get rid of it."

"Then why hasn't someone......" Eileen began.

"Because no one has any money," he interrupted her tetchily.

"School-teachers and priests are the only ones with money nowadays," he remarked caustically, getting off the tea chest to reach for a woodbine, and grumbling incessantly about his own misfortunes whilst he searched around for his matches.

"I'm stony broke in this place," he confided with deadly seriousness.

Eileen giggled. Mike was a perpetual moaner. He hadn't changed. While they chatted, her thoughts never once strayed from the 'For sale' sign in the garden. She had a whole weekend to consider the crazy plan taking shape in her head, but first she must beg a bed from the miller's wife who lived on the opposite side of the river.

"There will always be a bed for you," Nellie had assured her tearfully the day she left the village.

She floated worriedly from one idea to another, each with its own momentary insurmountable problems, and a new day was dawning when she finally reached a decision. She would buy *'Cois Abhainn'*. This impulsive act could drain her resources alarmingly, she acknowledged. But she still had her job and with stringent management and determination she would survive.

She jumped out of bed hastily and ran to the window to look once again at the house standing alone and forlorn in the early morning light, convinced that with her own particular flair for decorating she could transform it into the warm and friendly home it had once been. The prospect of returning to *Cois Abhainn* for Christmas and Easter and the long summer holidays was both joyous and exhilarating.

Happily for her, Mike's predictions proved correct and she boarded the bus two months later for a return trip to the house of her dreams. She bought it 'chape', acutely aware of the hard slog and expense involved in its restoration, but nothing would deter her.

Staring unseeing at the passing scenery she blushed, remembering the surge of excitement that shot through her when Mike mentioned casually that Jimmy Morahan next door had never got married.

Jimmy who had professed undying love and promised he would wait for ever for her, but contact had flickered and died over the years.

"County Mayo here I come, right back where I started from," her heart sang happily as the bus spat and spluttered on its way.

It was good to be going home at last.

# The Ireland We Remember

*Connemara landscape*

CHAPTER 20

# Tuesday For Wealth

*"Monday for health
Tuesday for wealth
Wednesday's the best day of all
Thursday for losses,
Friday for crosses, an'...
Saturday's no day at all."*

THE WORDS KEPT GOING round and round in Mary Kate's head. Would she be wealthy, she wondered. Not that it mattered. Money wasn't important, but it could 'come in very handy' she thought dreamily. Shrove Tuesday, in February 1940, the day before Lent began, was going to be her wedding day. Couples were not joined in matrimony during the Lenten period, as this was a six-week stretch of prayer and fast and abstinence. Therefore, all celebrations, particularly weddings, were put on hold until Easter week.

Mary Kate's bridegroom-to-be didn't fancy postponing their nuptials for so long, just in case the bride had second thoughts, and he certainly had no intention of letting her slip through his fingers now. She was the nicest thing that ever happened to him.

Her mother had hoped for a Wednesday wedding - the best day of all, while her father 'wasn't too pushed' provided that it wasn't on a Friday, "because ya couldn't even ate a bit o'mate wit yer dinner," to which his wife retorted, "ya think o'nothin' but yer belly."

It all began for Mary Kate when her Uncle Mick arranged a meeting between herself and Joe Murphy from Brownsisland, seven miles away. Joe was on the lookout for a woman, Uncle told her, an' he was well worth considerin'.

"There's no wan in the house, only 'imself," he repeated over and over in deadly earnestness. "No girl in her right mind would turn down the chance to begin her married life without in-laws or grandparents lookin' down 'er neck. An' fots more, he added, warming to his subject, ye'd be yer own boss. Joe promised to buy ya a new bike to come and go as ya like."

Sounded good to Mary Kate, but her father, always one to have the last word, had some reservations about Joe, following a few not-so-discreet enquiries 'on his daughter's behalf' "A great catch," he acknowledged thoughtfully, "nice bit o'land. Could be better stocked, though. Livin' on 'is own.... but a bit wild when he has the few pints on 'im, d'see."

There! He had said it at last. He had done his duty, completely ignoring the fact that he himself was partial to much more than 'a few', whenever the opportunity arose. But Mary Kate was paying no attention to his oul' guff.

"I'd marry 'im if t'was only for his lovely head o' hair," she declared defiantly after her first meeting with Joe, when Uncle took him to her parents house to introduce him 'an' discuss a bit o' business'.

The 'business' was all about the dowry of this extremely good-looking twenty-four year old girl. A slim, feisty, energetic, dark-haired lass who was happy helping her father on their small farm in the quiet backwater of Corribglen, where young men were 'as scarce as hens teeth', due to the fact that, one by one, they took the boat to England at sixteen and seventeen years of age, and sadly, most of them never returned.

Actually, Mary Kate was quite excited about meeting Joe Murphy, and he didn't disappoint her. She just loved his lazy lop-sided grin and his smouldering blue eyes that clearly said 'yer a bit of allright yerself'.

He was a thirty-year old, brown-haired, six footer who dressed well and had shoes so shiny you could almost see yourself in them. She knew her father was thinking 'A good-for-nothin'' as he eyeballed the shoes. Daddy liked his farmers to look the part, smell the part and act the part. But, after that first meeting, she didn't care much what he thought. Joe looked absolutely gorgeous to her. He had that certain something that set him apart from the men she usually saw at Mass on Sundays, who suddenly seemed dull and boring in comparison.

She could only hope that he was not as embarrassed as she herself was, one week later, when the thorny subject of her dowry was introduced. How could they discuss her as if she wasn't there?

The barely imperceptible wink from Joe in her direction said 'Hold on', when she would gladly have thrown a bucket of cold water on Uncle Mick's head.... and her father's also. This match-making thing was not her particular forte, but she knew that without it she would never have met Joe, and so far, she definitely liked what she saw.

He called to her home three Sunday nights in succession, and on the fourth night when all was finalised, and Mary Kate had said 'Yes', she walked with Joe to the front gate, knowing instinctively that her mother was peeping out from behind the curtains to satisfy herself that he wasn't taking liberties before he put the wedding ring on her finger. Truth to tell, Mary Kate wouldn't have objected if he put his arm around her - just to make her feel special on a very special night - but he didn't. Instead, he surprised her by saying softly, unexpectedly, with a wealth of love in his eyes,

"Ya look so beautiful to me. I'm no good at flowery speeches, but I'm the proudest man in the parish tonight. Ya won't let them change yer mind, will ya," he whispered anxiously, jerking his head towards the kitchen window where Mary Kate's mother remained vigilant.

"No fear o' that," she assured him earnestly. She could honestly say she thought Joe was beautiful also, but she was too shy to reveal her innermost feelings, and, furthermore, it was well-known that some men considered girls 'a bit brassy' if they spoke about such things. Hopefully, Joe Murphy was not one of them. He's simply gorgeous, she told herself over and over, and marvelled at her good fortune. Why a good-looker like him would choose HER, when he could have the pick o' the parish, was beyond her. Little did she realise that Joe was thinking how fortunate HE was to have found HER. All in all, matchmaking had some good points, she decided, and silently thanked Uncle Mick for his good taste in men.

Shrove Tuesday dawned bright and crisp with more than a hint of frost on the ground, but it mattered not one whit.

'Monday for health, Tuesday for wealth.'

Mary Kate's heart sang, as she rushed around the house doing the usual morning chores. Her father obviously had a change of mind during the matchmaking period, and now assured her that Joe was a "damn fine fella, an' the few pints never did anyone any harm".

He was so pleased 'for 'er gettin' a man' that he began to dance a little quick-step around the kitchen, singing at the top of his voice,

*'Step it out Mary, my fine daughther,*
*Step it out Mary, if you can,*
*Step it out Mary, my fine daughther,*
*Show yer legs to the country man'*

Mary Kate aimed at the back of his head with the dishcloth, and she didn't miss. Then both of them tip-toed around the kitchen table, laughing helplessly as they danced.

He indulged in a bit of self-pity later. Who would feed the calves and the geese and the hens tomorrow morning? More importantly, who would have his breakfast on the table at 7 am?

Try doin' it yourself, Mary Kate thought, without much sympathy, knowing that her mother would be ready and willing to wait on him all day. He was only fifty-seven, for God's sake, and as sprightly as any forty-year old in the village.

"Peata mór," she mouthed at him with a cheeky grin and continued with her chores.

She washed her hair with rain-water from the barrel under the thatch, giving it a lovely silky-soft look that emphasized her natural waves and curls, and finally, she dressed up in her royal blue costume, matched with a navy hat and navy high-heeled shoes, hoping with all her heart that Joe Murphy would feel proud of her when they met at the altar rails at three o'clock.

One hour later they walked down the aisle as man and wife. No photographs, no fuss, just jovial congratulations and handshakes from the small group around them. Cameras were practically non-existent in those days, but the newly weds could dress up in their wedding finery later in the week and cycle into town to have a photograph taken by a professional photographer if they so wished.

The 'draggin', which consisted of two hackney cars, crawled away from the chapel with seven people, plus the driver, in each car - all sitting on each others knees - but no one complained. They tied oul' buckets and tin cans at the back, and rattled their way to Joe's home, seven miles away, where the neighbours had gathered and celebrations began in style, continuing well into sunrise next morning.

Few were sober but all were maudlin when they had downed at least the sixth 'one for the road', declaring stoutly that Joe Murphy was the luckiest man alive to have got such a lovely bride, though some with daughters of their own privately thought he didn't need to go half so far for a woman.

Mary Kate's father blew his nose loudly and reminded her to come home for 'the month's visit', which had her in tears despite her best efforts, as she suddenly realised this was the first time she was separated from parents and home. Back then, it was customary for brides to refrain from visiting the family home for one month after marriage, and this was strictly adhered to in most places until the early fifties.

Breaking with tradition brought bad luck, her parents warned, when she announced cockily that she didn't believe in any of that nonsense, but standing there in the crisp morning air, she knew with certainty that despite her reluctance to accept old traditions, she would never try to change things.

Her mother would still be tucked up in bed in Corribglen, she thought tearfully, and resentment flared briefly, remembering all the useless coaxing and cajoling to encourage her to attend the wedding.

"Someone has to wait at home an' mind the house," she insisted stubbornly, refusing to budge.

But Mary Kate was well aware that mothers rarely, if ever, attended their children's marriages. It was not 'the done thing', and oft times young brides made a hasty exit from home with tear-stained cheeks while their mothers remained indoors and cried. Just as Mary Kate was crying because she couldn't go home for a full month.

That was the moment she felt Joe's arm around her waist - so protective, so secure. Suddenly, she felt she could endure anything with Joe by her side, and her worries began to fade like mist in the morning sun. Then panic took over. What was he thinking of in front of that drunken lot, for God's sake? She tried to break free, but Joe held her fast in a vice-like grip that sent excitement coursing through her veins.

There was devilment in his eyes as he held her close, and taking her hand, he placed it firmly around his own waist, much to the astonishment of his audience who staggered down the boreen convinced that Joe Murphy was definitely a bit 'on the wild side' when he had 'the dhrink on 'im'.

Folding her tenderly in his arms, he whispered softly, "Never mind that lot. I'm so proud and happy today. I'm goin' to love you forever, I promise."

Happiness bubbled up inside her as they walked back to the house with arms entwined, on that unforgettable first morning as Mr and Mrs Joe Murphy.

*'Monday for health,*
*Tuesday for wealth......'*

They were rich beyond compare.

*'Step it out Mary, my fine Daughter'*

# CHAPTER 21

# Only an Irishman's Dream

"YOU'RE GOING TO DO WHAT?" Betty stared wide-eyed and open-mouthed at her husband, a look of utter bewilderment spreading across her normally serene face.

Joe was well aware that it was not going to be easy to confront his wife with his proposal, and had waited for weeks until she was, he hoped, in a receptive frame of mind.

"Have you gone mad?" Betty demanded, the mutinous tightening of her mouth signalling storm clouds ahead.

"To think of going back to Ireland is bad enough," she burst out, "but to buy a PUB, Joe! How daft can you get? For God's sake, you'd be your own best customer, and well you know it," she flung at him with increasing annoyance. "That's what I'd call puttin' the fox in charge o' the hen-house," she added with more than a trace of sarcasm in every word.

Joe managed to interrupt her outburst at last, hastening to reassure her on a subject that was, for her, both painful and embarrassing.

"I'm doing it for the Holy Souls," Joe insisted as he sipped his last drink on Shrove Tuesday night and the last cigarette was tossed dramatically into the bin.

"When I get my own pub there'll be no more drinkin'," Joe assured her solemnly. "I'll never touch a drop again and that's a sacred promise," he vowed, purposely avoiding the withering look in her eye, as she heatedly recalled all the Lenten fasts made with such conviction and abandoned within hours through obvious lack of will power.

Neither the Holy Souls nor the obligatory Lenten impositions ever gained much from Joe's erratic abstentions. But this time he was going to succeed. The days of intemperance were over. Steadfast resolutions were poured into his wife's sceptical ear as he pleaded for tolerance and support.

A life-time of dreams depended on his commitment.

Joe could never remember the exact moment when the idea of returning to Ireland filtered through his mind, light and flimsy as gossamer at first, but sufficient to raise some doubts about his sanity nonetheless.

It was a gradual intrusion into his life over many years, during which time he alternated between nurturing and discarding what seemed both rational and absurd, according to his mood.

Perhaps the fact that he was comfortable in Manchester for thirty-five years caused him to have certain reservations about venturing into the unknown. He had built up a thriving business in civil engineering, studying long hours at night-school in his youth until he finally reached his goal.

At fifty-four Joe was a self-made man. He was a hefty, brown-haired entrepreneur who neither looked nor felt a day over forty. He still possessed the same single-mindedness which enabled him to brush obstacles aside and obtain his objectives throughout his working life. A pub would be ideal to activate his enthusiasm once again, he decided.

Betty eyed him balefully as she remembered another 'Lenten fast', of a more intimate nature, broken on Saint Patrick's Day – 'the mid-term break, Joe called it' - and resulting in two Christmas babies while Manchester froze in twelve inches of snow.

"How the heck do I get you to the hospital?" Joe panicked.

"Hire a donkey and pretend we're off to Bethlehem", Betty had snapped waspishly.

Joe's promises could hardly be relied upon she thought sourly, as he wheedled and cajoled and sang the praises of 'the green, green, grass of home'. Betty sharply reminded him of the many unfortunates who had returned to Ireland when the reversal of the migration flows first began, only to find themselves totally unable to adjust.

"Damn glad they were to pack their bags and hightail it back to John Bull", she sniffed contemptuously. She was not going to make it easy for him now, she decided. She refused to be forced into a decision overnight.

Betty loved her own Mancunian lifestyle. She was actively involved with the amateur dramatic group in the Irish Centre, and was loudly acclaimed as a brilliant actress. Her outstanding performance as leading lady in 'The Inebriate Woman' was a tribute to her considerable talents. The group's members would deem it unthinkable to tread the boards without their guiding light, the vivacious fair-haired Betty Mulvey. Joe rarely attended their shows. Prancing around on stage unnerved him, he insisted, retreating to his own particular peace-haven with a Jameson for company.

It would be difficult for Betty to wrench herself away from Manchester, and return to Ireland in pursuit of a dream. Joe, however, had no such qualms. He had worked all his life for the day he could return. He didn't expect a positive reply from his wife immediately, but he could wait. He always managed to change her mind eventually...

The fasting was usually over on Ash Wednesday for Joe. He was back in his local as always for a 'quick one' and a 'few smokes'. A hardworking man such as he could not be expected to do penance. It was a useless exercise anyway. The Holy Souls were unlikely to be in a position to return the favour.... ever. But this time it was going to be different.

"Give it time Joe, and you won't miss it one bit," Betty encouraged soothingly.

Joe groaned inwardly at the thought.

For the next few months he was doggedly faithful to his promise 'never to touch a drop again', and endured daily anguish as his work-mates updated him with tales of numerous pints consumed nightly with relish. Despite their jovial efforts to weaken his resolve, Joe persevered. The keys to his dream pub hung precariously on his vows. The days melted into weeks and even Betty became proud of his staying-power.

Months of pub-hunting ceased as Joe's dream became a reality and plans progressed for their momentous move to Ireland. The Mulvey house buzzed with activity as the scheduled departure day drew near. Joe secretly detested all the upheaval and packing associated with moving house, and for one wild unfettered moment in the midst of it all, he would have given his soul to dash to the local tavern and bury his face in a pint of deliciously cool beer. The thought brought a thin film of sweat to his forehead, while his suddenly parched mouth ached with longing, but temptation passed when Betty called loudly,

"Gimme a hand to move this thing, Joe," as she picked her way to the old piano and began to play, *"It was only an Irishman's Dream"*, with a look in her eye that suggested she read his thoughts correctly.

Their newly acquired public house on the western seaboard overlooking the pounding Atlantic was both impressive and welcoming. From the front windows, they had a breathtaking view of a greeny-blue sea with its frothy waves gently slapping the coastline and curling possessively around the slimy rocks beneath them.

It was all rather strange at first. Standing behind the counter pulling pints for others was a new experience for Joe, but he gained vital knowledge through the learning process. Certain skills were required to 'pull a good pint' or to put a 'good head' on it, and these were accomplished under the expert tuition of the veteran drinkers of the establishment. However, with time, all this educational stuff became extremely stress-inducing, and Joe drifted into the habit of treating himself to a 'few small ones' with the after-hours patrons who were reluctant to leave without one more for the road.

"A night cap will help you to wind down after a long day," they assured him.

Joe echoed their sentiments entirely.

The 'small ones' consumed with reckless abandon had a remarkably calming influence, particularly as Betty's amazingly keen sense of smell seemed to have deserted her completely. Joe was relieved. She deserved better than fretting over trivial matters. After all, she attended to the serious end of the business, rising each morning to have the premises fresh and clean for opening time. Joe could hear her downstairs banging bottles and barrels while he nursed his thumping head under the blankets.

"Nourishment is what I need, not punishment," he moaned, when Betty rapped on the ceiling with the sweeping brush to wake him up.

To his utter dismay, he discovered soon afterwards that his wife was sneaking vodka to the kitchen. Betty, who had never touched a drop in her life, began knocking off generous measures of the stuff nightly. She interrupted his cosy sessions with the boys, insisting on joining them, while she staggered across the floor and invited the men to dance with a 'come-hither' look in her dreamy eyes.

*'An' we'll all meet tonight,* (she belted out)
*An' we'll sing as loud as we can,*
*Of an island so green,*
*That can only be seen,*
*Through the eyes of an Irishman.'*

Once, she attempted an elaborate curtsey in front of Joe, lost her balance, and sank to the floor in a pathetic little heap.

"Cripes, you're stoned," Joe gasped, trying to move her limp form away from prying eyes. Sweat ran down his face from sheer embarrassment.

"Great pair o' legs," muttered one of his cronies. Joe's rage boiled over. Well, that lot just had their last gawk or his name wasn't Joe Mulvey. Great pair o' legs, indeed!

"Ye'll be out that door at closing time tomorrow night," he swore under his breath, glad to be able to vent his anger on others.

He was unable to stomach it all. A drunken woman he could not abide, especially when it was Betty. He pleaded, coaxed, went down on his knees almost, but she was oblivious to it all.

Soon their positions reversed. Betty no longer rushed down to commence her early morning chores, and Joe was forced to accept total responsibility for the day to day affairs of the bar. He was on his own now, he realised, and there could be no place in his life for drink if he wished to succeed in this new venture. Grudgingly, he admitted to himself that he was close to ruining all he had ever worked for. Close to being a failure...

'Damn glad they were to pack their bags...' Betty's words haunted him for days. Well, he'd show her! He'd be damned if he was going to hightail it back to John Bull, he told himself defiantly. The late night sessions were over forever, he vowed with grim determination, and for the first time in his life he kept his word……

Betty watched her husband as he climbed the stairs, having closed the pub on time for the past three months. Standing steady and erect she raised her glass and proposed a toast,

"To *'The Inebriate Woman'*, my forever friend," she whispered conspiratorially, emptying the remains of her tepid soda water into the kitchen sink. She smiled and turned out the lights, well pleased for having achieved yet another outstanding performance.

*The Ireland We Remember*

*The dream of a lifetime*

CHAPTER 22

# Home for Christmas

CATHERINE STARED AT THE supermarket windows with all its tinsel and imaginary snow piled against the corners of the window-panes.

"Is it Christmas?" She must have spoken aloud, she realised. The youth with the long hair strumming his guitar, just inches away from her, stopped playing and muttered, "Does it look like it?"

"Christmas is for giving," he said hopefully a moment later, but considering the fact that Catherine still hadn't taken in her garden chair from the back yard, where she 'holidayed' beneath an umbrella in August, it seemed almost immoral to think of Christmas or indeed giving.

She stood there in the pouring rain, the supermarket and its surroundings all fading into the background of her memory. Instead she could vividly see the grocery shop of her youth with the seed-loaves and barm-bracks, and the unforgettable smell of tea from the big tea-chest outside the counter. Catherine remembered the old shopkeeper well,

'Oul' John' as he was known to all the locals. He sold huge quantities of currants and big fat seed-raisins to the farmers wives in time for the Christmas baking spree, and they, in turn, looked forward to their annual 'Christmas Box', which consisted of mainly of tea, sugar and two red candles.

Considerable care was taken to provide a good solid meal on Christmas Eve, when everyone was starving after a day of fast and abstinence, not to mention the nerve-racking ordeal of going to the chapel to make a general confession in preparation for the birth of our Lord.

Rarely did the men partake in any of the festivities, apart from over-eating, Catherine recalled. Across the street a farmer stood by his car, hoping to sell the four turkeys he had displayed on the bonnet, awakening memories of the two Rhode-Island red cocks who enjoyed a longer-than-usual period with the hens, in order to fatten them up for Christmas. Her mother 'handled' them carefully, returning the best pair to the flock for extra feeding. Their more unfortunate brothers had got 'the chop', in honour of St. Martin.

Her mother also reared geese. Catherine knew her father would be loading them into the cart every Big Market Monday, the biggest and most important shopping day in the town before Christmas. She had abiding recollections of him returning home after dark each year, and her mother's sharp rebuke,

"Where were you until this hour?"

Catherine had to hold up the lantern to enable her father to undo the horse's harness, and release him from under the cart after a long day. She had learned to step aside nimbly when the horse, on sensing he was free, bolted from under the cart, released at last from being tied to a lamp-post for hours, while her father gargled the Christmas spirit in a near-by pub.

Years afterwards Catherine understood her mother's counting and re-counting of the 'goose money'. It was well calculated for weeks, but the actual amount she received from the man of the house fell far short of her expectations. A sharp exchange of words always followed, then deadly silence, broken only by the loud snores of 'himself' sleeping off his drink.

Catherine decided to walk to the bridge. She was cold and wet. The street and its people didn't exist. She was a young girl again...yes, there it was, straight ahead. It looked much wider now. Just as she was about to cross a policeman shouted,

"Don't cross there missus, you'll get run over."

She snorted. As if she didn't know every inch of that bridge! Whatever was he thinking of.

"You've been down in the snug again Sergeant," she said winking wickedly, "but your secret is safe with me. After all it is Christmas."

He looked at her curiously. She spoke as if she recognised him, but he was new to this area….

"Where are you heading for missus?" he asked, reaching out to take her arm.

She shrugged him off crossly. "As if you didn't know, Joe Brown. Bertie will be waiting for me down at the Old Mill."

The policeman smiled. Too many hot whiskeys, he had no doubt. He'd keep an eye on her.

Catherine trudged on. The bridge had railings now. You could look down at the river beneath, but she only saw the stone-built bridge of her youth, and re-lived again the climbing up and chasing along the top, when one slight shove could send you hurtling into the churning waters below.

"There must be a funeral," she thought, slightly nervous of attempting to cross over to the other side.

She re-traced her steps, feeling exhausted. She didn't notice the rain. Fairy-lights were switched on in the street. Fog and rain made them wink when she looked at them.

She was so pleased that people remembered to light their candles. She saw the lovely old thatched cottages with one of Oul John's candles in each window, to welcome the Baby Jesus on that blessed night.

Ahead of her, she could just about catch a glimpse of the chapel through the rain. She ambled on, commanding legs wobbly from fatigue to carry her a little bit further to the doorway. She sank into her customary place, the third seat from the altar. There was Oul' John kneeling at the crib. She'd go and wish him Happy Christmas when she stopped feeling so bone-weary.

A little girl walked towards the altar with a note in her hand. That would be her letter to Santy, Catherine decided. In days gone by, she would have re-written her own, nightly, right up to Christmas Eve when she placed it in her long black stocking beside the open fire. The fact that Santy managed to come down their narrow chimney always intrigued her. All the evidence was there in the morning…soot scraped down, and marks on the floor where a none-too-tidy Santy walked around in his snow-shoes. How clearly she recalled hearing him slip and slide his way down when she was six. She hid underneath the blankets, too scared to look. He never brought very much, but nothing could compare with the joy of ripping open her present, even if it contained no more than a few biscuits.

The chapel was decorated with holly, loaded down with red berries. Just as it always was. There was something ethereal about this holy place, she reflected, as she gazed in silent wonder at the golden glow from the candles on the altar. Then she nodded off to the sound of the most haunting of all Christmas hymns, *'Adeste Fidelus'*…She tried to sing but despite her best efforts the words failed to come out. The body heat of the people and the enchanting background music had their own effect on her weary limbs, and she sank into a deep slumber oblivious to everything around her.

Ages later, someone was tugging at her sleeve. She heard her grandson scolding her,

"You shouldn't have wandered off like that Gran. If I hadn't met the new policeman I wouldn't have found you tonight."

"Ah yes," she said, "Joe Brown. We've been friends for fifty-two years. We sang together in the church choir, I'll have you know."

"Where did you go anyway?" her grandson asked as he helped her to her feet.

"I was home for Christmas," she smiled, "and it was so beautiful. Nothing has changed at all."

Down on the street corner near the bridge, the new policeman strolled up and down watching Christmas shoppers jostle each other on the pavements, whilst his thoughts kept wandering back to the little old lady who called him Joe Brown.

Strange. She couldn't have known him, could she? She had called him Sergeant. His father was once Sergeant Joe Brown in a beautiful, albeit remote part of the country. He had regaled his family on countless occasions with stories of his youth when he was an integral part of a lively and amicable community.

Young Joe, his son, had vivid recollections of his father's eulogies of a certain young soprano named Catherine, who remained his close friend until he was posted to another town, eighty miles away. Communication wavered and died over the years, but Sergeant Brown never forgot that young girl with the wonderful voice and her little dog, Bertie, under her arm wherever she went. Would it be too much to hope this good lady's name might be Catherine also…?

"You must have learned at this stage in your life that you shouldn't jump to conclusions," was his father's indifferent reply when his son found a moment to telephone and acquaint him with the strange encounter.

"She's goofy, Pop," his son declared, ever so slightly aggrieved that his 'discovery' evoked little or no response from his father who was spending Christmas with him. However, young Joe was well aware that despite the fact that his father was now retired, he still had the urge to 'sniff out' the unconventional or the off-beat, and curiosity, if nothing else, would be the stimulant to activate his interest.

Replacing the receiver, Joe was satisfied that even as he spoke, his father was already reaching for his coat, and strolling casually from the other end of town to privately suss out this individual who professed to know Sergeant Joe Brown.

Back on the beat, Joe junior retraced his steps and reached the chapel just as the congregation was spilling out onto the street after midnight Mass. The choir were taking up their positions on the steps for their annual carol-singing, and the whole scene was one of hand-shakes and good wishes. From the rear of the crowd the young policeman saw the old lady, now looking surprisingly perky and not quite so old, emerge from the chapel on her grandson's arm. She pushed her way towards the choir just as his astonished father moved forward and said softly, "Catherine?"

She stared blankly for a moment, then grasped his hands, as delightful recognition set her animated features aglow.

"Joe Brown, you've come back," she whispered joyously. Together, as the music began, they joined with the choir to treat a hushed and receptive gathering to a superb intonation of *'Silent Night'*.

This was without doubt going to be a very happy Christmas for ex-Sergeant Joe Brown and his long-lost somewhat scatty friend, Catherine.

# Anne Morrin

*The elegant young lady of the '30's*

CHAPTER 23

# Pamela's Pride

Pamela Dawson lived in a fairytale world of her own. She excelled at playing 'Lady of the Manor', sometimes to the embarrassment of her youngest daughter, Judith, who was well aware that friends hid their amusement when her mother got carried away with tales of former glory and wealth. Every conversation was sprinkled with lords, ladies, peers, admirals and generals, and while her friends tolerated her harmless delusions of grandeur, they also wished she would come back and live in the real world.

"We were disgustingly rich, my dears," she told them now, stifling a rising sob, "and look at us today - reduced to this hovel."

This 'hovel' was the house she had lived in for years. The ancestral home of the Dawson's, set in idyllic surroundings on the shores of Lough Corrib in County Mayo, and restored at considerable expense by her beloved husband, Richard. It was still in reasonably good condition, but Pamela loved to dramatize.

"For goodness sake, Mother," Judith interrupted her gently, "thousands of people wouldn't consider an eighteenth century mansion with all its period pieces still intact, exactly a 'hovel', would they?"

"They are not the Dawsons," her mother replied with great majesty, squelching any further argument in the presence of her friends.

Judith wished their guests would leave. She had a busy day ahead. Ever since her father's death three years ago, she managed the one-hundred-and-fifty-acre Dawson estate single-handedly, except for the occasional help of a local yard boy. Her mother, and her sister, Karen, entertained friends, played golf, and shopped in all the best places, presenting ongoing financial problems for Judith. Those two ladies, so indulged and so protected while Pamela's husband was alive, were still unable to face reality. Dear, dear Richard took care of all the monetary business, telling his wife not to worry her pretty little head about such things. Anything concerning money was met with vagueness personified, and Pamela was always happy to oblige her unflappable Richard.

It was a wonderful affluent world they lived in, but recently Judith was stressing that spending-cuts were a necessary evil to weather the bad patch the estate was experiencing for some time. It was damnable, Pamela moaned theatrically, dabbing her eyes with a dainty square of linen and lace, as she bade farewell to her distinguished guests.

Pamela and her eldest daughter were exactly alike, or at least as alike as any two women separated by twenty-six years could be. Both were tall, brown-eyed, brown-haired ladies, with creamy-golden tans, a tendency towards big bones, and a penchant for the dramatic in both dress and manner. Twenty-four year old Judith took after her father with honey-blonde hair and beautiful blue eyes set in a small heart-shaped face. She was a firm favourite with the local people, while her mother and sister hobnobbed with the upper classes only.

They weren't very helpful now, Judith thought wearily. They could, at least, restrict their spending and their lavish lifestyle until this recession blew over. She lamented the fact that their allowance was not as generous as in previous years, and for the umpteenth time she fervently wished her father had left the Dawson estate to Pamela and Karen, and left her to her own devices.

Actually, her father did bequeath a substantial sum of money to his wife and daughter, most of which was spent unwisely. Huge chunks were hacked away with scant regard for their rapidly diminishing inheritance. It really was too bad of Richard to have passed the property on to their youngest-born, Pamela thought frustratedly. Preservation of the Dawson estate was all very fine, but starvation was quite another thing.

"I must say you really are stretching this economy thing much too far, dear," Pamela remarked crossly, as Judith sat down to pore over her accounts when their guests departed. Pacing the drawing-room floor agitatedly, she stopped abruptly beside Judith and announced with solemn finality,

"Karen must find herself a wealthy husband. We need money to release us from this awful poverty trap."

"Don't exaggerate, Mother," Judith pleaded, hiding a smile. "You know perfectly well we'll get by if we take care."

But Pamela refused to be consoled, and pressed ahead with plans for the salvation of the family fortunes.

"Karen is so beautiful," she mused. "I feel confident that many men will vie with each other for her affections."

Suddenly she brightened, and Judith waited, aware that her mother was putting her rescue package together.

"We'll throw the biggest party ever," she decided joyfully, "and invite all the most eligible bachelors in the county. That way, Karen can pick and choose."

"Will I get to pick and choose also?" Judith laughed outright at her mother's scheming face, before Pamela reminded her sharply,

"You, my dear, have your horses and your land, but Karen is utterly reliant on her beauty. The dear child has nothing more to offer."

She was striving for composure, and Judith hastily suggested an early night before she trotted out her customary grievance that Judith had all, while she and Karen were beggars. Judith laughed helplessly as she returned to her books. The biggest party ever? Some hope!

It was abundantly clear that Judith would not be the one to rescue them from financial disaster, Pamela reflected ruefully. If ever she married, to would be to some rough welly-shod farmer, whose only thoughts would be for his bulls and cows. Pamela's nose twitched in revulsion. Take for example, Grant Ormsby, that obnoxious young man who was installed as caretaker over at Mellory Hall just a year ago. Judith was quite besotted from their very first meeting. It was most disturbing, but much more unnerving was the fact that Karen was also captivated by his stunning good looks and his powerfully built well-tanned body.

"What a gorgeous hunk, Mummy," Karen enthused. "He's such a magnificent animal. I'm just crazy about him."

"The brute is penniless," Pamela snorted. "Don't waste silly schoolgirl crushes on his type. Mr Perfect will come your way very soon, dear." She patted her arm reassuringly.

As if there were not enough problems with Judith already, she thought uneasily, now Karen has fallen under his spell also. What has that man got, anyway? Cheek, for one thing, Pamela felt sure. Driving around in Lady Mellory's Bentley with a smirk on his face as if he owned the Hall. Indeed, she felt duty-bound to put that 'magnificent animal' firmly in his place the next time he called to take Judith out.

"I hope the owners of Mellory Hall pay you well, young man," she snapped at the first opportunity. "You seem to have taken on quite a lot............for a mere caretaker, that is."

"I have indeed, Ma'am," he replied unruffled, "but I love my work and the scenery here is just breathtaking."

"Does Lady Mellory allow all the staff to borrow her Bentley?" Pamela wanted to know.

"No. Only me. I'm her favourite little boy," he told her poker-faced. Was he laughing at her? She caught a glint of amusement in his eye, and had a sudden urge to slap his face. Bad-mannered lout.

Judith must be persuaded to end her relationship with Grant Ormsby immediately, Pamela decided, but the totally unexpected announcement some days later, of her daughter's engagement, dashed all her hopes. Whatever was the silly child thinking of? Young love was incredibly sweet, she remembered, and Judith would probably have that, but precious little else.

To add to her dismay, Grant's parents were coming to Mellory Hall to meet and celebrate with their future daughter-in-law, of whom their son always spoke so lovingly. They might understand her anxiety, and hopefully discourage those naive youngsters. In any case, the Dawson estate could ill-afford a hanger-on in its present predicament, she thought with some satisfaction.

The look of sheer incredulity on Pamela's face was a sight to behold the day Grant came round to introduce his mother and stepfather, Lord and Lady Mellory. That haughty lady cringed with embarrassment when she recalled his amusement days earlier. Why had she just assumed he was a wretched caretaker, but never asked? She had reprimanded the only son of upper-class titled people, who were filthy rich to boot............

That last thought cheered her immensely, and come sundown she was vigorously planning her 'Mother of the Bride' wardrobe, together with a list of all the 'best' people in the county. She herself would mingle with their wedding guests in the exalted company of Lord and Lady Mellory. It would definitely be the 'Wedding of the West'.

The young lovers smiled indulgently as Pamela dreamed on, and longing for a little privacy, they strolled happily to a secluded corner of the garden, where they melted into each other's arms, with stars in their eyes and a world of love in their hearts that no amount of riches could buy.

*Waiting patiently for their early morning canter*

CHAPTER 24

# Love or Land

Tessie blinked non-stop in the harsh glare of the early April sunshine, and shaded her eyes with the soft kid gloves that were part of every discerning young lady's outfit in the forties.

It all seemed so unreal. She stole a glance at Jamie and got the distinct impression that his brand new shirt and tie were far too tight. The urge to move closer and whisper, 'Will ye open the top button before ye choke' was almost irresistible. But not to-day. Not in front of the handful of pious people who usually attended early morning Mass. Onlookers made Jamie very uncomfortable.

They lived in the same house for fifteen years. As a youngster, Tessie helped her Aunt Bridget to wash, clean and cook for him, in addition to assisting him with little jobs on the farm, after school, in the evenings. There was nothing she didn't know about Jamie. He was like a big brother. One of those who wouldn't be 'seen dead' with her in public in their 'know-all' distant school-days. Lads were branded as 'sissies' if they hung around with their sisters in bygone times, and Jamie let everyone know he was no sissy.

He was always ahead or behind, but never alongside of her, as they cycled to Sunday Mass, when they were old enough to get two second-hand bikes that were constantly having flat tyres. Jamie pedalled steadily, with exaggerated confidence, to the chapel gate where the local lads congregated, and pretended to be all alone. Tessie couldn't care less, she told herself defiantly. She eyeballed the lads while she leaned her bike against a yew-tree, and blushed daintily when they winked or whistled.

For some inexplicable reason this seemed to ruffle Jamie's temper, and Tessie strode in to Mass with her nose in the air, delighted to get even with 'misther-smarty-pants who thinks he knows ever'thin'.

But that was all of fifteen years ago. She smiled now, remembering what a cheeky eight-year old tomboy she had been, when her parents sent her to live with Aunt Bridget and her husband, Miko Moran, who lived on a twenty acre farm on a hill-top overlooking Silver Bay, near Lough Corrib. They had no children of their own, and Tessie's unexpected arrival livened up their days in no uncertain way.

Miko was not too impressed. He suspected Tessie's parents gave them the child, not out of the goodness of their hearts, but with their eye on the farm for that same child in later years. Well... he'd pip them at the post, he thought mischievously, and six months later he had coaxed his own nine-year old nephew, Jamie, to Silver Bay, 'where he's badly wanted to gimme a hand with'e sheep', he insisted stubbornly, when Bridget tried, in vain, to persuade him to change his mind. But Miko was adamant, and his nephew, quiet, unassuming Jamie, was transported on the carrier of his father's bike to the Moran farm-house, where he met Tessie for the first time in his young life.

In those days it was not at all unusual for parents to 'give away' a child to an elderly childless relative. Not entirely because that relative pined for children, but mainly because it relieved the burden for the parents, who then had one less mouth to feed, in an already stretched-to-the-limit household.

Relations were not the only ones to 'take in' a child. Oft times an elderly couple 'took a shine' to a neighbours child …. preferably a boy …. and showered him with love and affection. He wallowed in their undivided attention, sitting in the hob, beside the open fire, while he stuffed himself with potatoes and butter that never tasted half so good at home. He helped with little jobs around the house, and when the rain came he slept comfortably for the night in the old settle-bed in the kitchen. Gradually, he became a vital part of their lives, and 'stayed for good' when school years were left behind.

Hostility reared its ugly head within days of Jamie's arrival at Silver Bay. He could feel Tessie's displeasure almost as if she feared he would supplant her. They squabbled and screamed over crayons and pencils while he walked to school with her, and it certainly didn't help to have 'that oul' Bridget' wagging her bony finger, commanding him to 'mind Tessie now, on the way', even though there was nothing on the narrow boreen but a few stray sheep.

He told himself he hated her when she lashed out at him. Nevertheless, there was something very endearing about her – something his young mind failed to understand – and he was irresistibly drawn back, time and again, for more punishment.

"Cry-babby," she spat at him, spoiling for fight, but he always ignored her, aware that her fiery temper would cool in minutes, and an amicable silence would descend on them for a very brief period.

Bridget and Miko looked on in admiration when tempers flared once again while the children's home-work was in progress, and were convinced that 'our two young wans' were the brightest and best in the west of Ireland.

All too soon the school years were over, and their squally childhood became a dim and distant memory. As teenagers, both realised there was very little future for them in Silver Bay, but neither would think of leaving, due to well-intentioned parental pressure from both sides, on that particular issue. They were totally dependant on their relatives, financially, and were it not for the old couple's pension, and a meagre income from the farm, they would have been compelled to emigrate like many of their age-group.

Any reference to that subject usually provoked an angry outburst from Miko, and as the months rolled into years, the secret thoughts that either might have harboured, albeit vaguely, about following in the footsteps of their schoolmates, faded into obscurity.

Little changes that gradually became bigger ones, crept stealthily into the Moran household with time. Miko took to staying indoors for long periods, rarely venturing out 'to give a hand' as he was wont to do. Arthritis was slowing him down considerably, much to his annoyance, especially when he was overcome with an overwhelming longing to climb once again to the top of the hill overlooking the Corrib, and watch the boats cruising in the tranquil waters of the bay beneath him.

Tessie could never remember when, exactly, she first became aware that Jamie was growing into a fine young man, as Aunt Bridget described him, and the timid young 'brother' was disappearing with their youth. Like Miko's arthritis, the change crept in ever so slowly, and went unnoticed for the most part, until such times as a farm problem arose, and it was left to Jamie to sort it out. He always ensured that Tessie, who was steadily blossoming into a vivacious young lady, had an input into every decision, knowing he could rely on her explicitness to guide him through some difficult times.

Tessie could not contemplate life without Jamie now. It would be very dull indeed if he was not there, but she would never, ever admit it. Him an' his Cary Grant good looks, an' the local lassies makin' eyes at him. She sniffed contemptuously at the thought, tossing her mane of curly brown hair off her shoulder, with her usual 'see if I care' dismissive gesture.

Jamie, for his part, kept his thoughts and his feelings well under control, and while he longed to get closer to her, he invariably backed off, convinced that she would laugh at his notions and make him look foolish.

Nevertheless, they were a good team, and worked well together, being of one mind about most things. They were determined, despite scrimping and scraping, to make the farm viable, forever hoping for a more productive new year.

Miko was well aware that Jamie was becoming increasingly dependent on Tessie as the days went by. A chip off the old block, he reckoned, remembering the days when he, himself, invented all sorts of excuses to persuade Bridget to assist him in the fields. He laughed heartily now at his little deceptions, and could recall with clarity their shared peace and contentment, as they rested in the shade beneath the old stone wall, with nothing to disturb the stillness except the twittering of the birds in the nearby white-thorn bushes.

"This is the nearest to Heaven we'll ever get," he'd mutter drowsily, before he succumbed to temptation and lay down for his daily cat-nap.

Shared peace and contentment? Sure-fire ingredients for a happy marriage, his thoughts rambled on, an' hadn't he fifty years of experience to prove it?

"That pair out there haven't a clue fot they're missin'," he burst out, pushing the cat off his lap in exasperation, "an' it's time someone talked sense into them. Anyone can see they're two of a kind. They just need a push in the right direction, an' I'm the man to do it," he told Bridget with great modesty.

Bridget, however, had reservations about interfering in the lives of the 'young wans'.

"If there's no 'spark' after all their years together, ye can forget about ye'r match-makin'," she snapped, clearly unimpressed with Miko's great plans to bring 'that pair to their senses.'

But despite his wife's misgivings, his meddlesome mind went into overdrive as he carefully hatched his plot. He made a will, leaving all he possessed to Jamie and Tessie equally. One of the stipulations in that all-important document required the joining together in matrimony of James Moran and Teresa Carroll, in order to inherit his or her share of the property. The Carrolls wouldn't have it all their own way, he thought gleefully, rubbing his bony hands together, and the Moran name would survive for another generation.

Furthermore, it was Miko's earnest wish that the marriage take place within a year, and the young couple must continue to reside in the Moran farmhouse, with himself and Bridget, and care for them in their impending twilight years........

Tessie roused herself from her reverie, and shaded her eyes once again from the sharp early morning sunshine. She looked into Jamie's smiling face as they stood outside the Church door, and could scarcely believe that one hour earlier, at 8 o'clock Mass, Jamie had placed a gold wedding-band on her finger, while the Priest solemnly pronounced them man and wife.

Self-conscious as usual, Jamie evaded inquisitive eyes, and guided Tessie across the Church yard to collect their bikes and head for home. Once out of earshot it was almost as if he could no longer contain himself. Words rushed out as he whispered emotionally,

"For fifteen years it was like we we're joined at the hip, an' to-day we're joined at the heart. It's the loveliest day of my life. How about you, Mrs. Moran?"

"Same here," Tessie assured him happily.

Shared peace and contentment …….. They would have that and much more.

# Anne Morrin

*Love conquers all*

CHAPTER 25

# Backup To The Stars

IN 1951 MUCH WAS written in the papers to herald the arrival of John Wayne and Maureen O'Hara for the making of that never-to-be-forgotten movie, 'The Quiet Man' at Cong in Co. Mayo, but perhaps not quite enough coverage was given to the experts - the advance team - without whose dedicated work the movie might not have been so successful.

This team of technicians, cameramen, prop-men, sound-men, make-up artists, wardrobe supervisors and numerous other professional men and women arrived ahead of the film stars and worked steadily in the vicinity of the castle and Cong, and various participating locations, to have the groundwork sorted out when the cast arrived at Ashford Castle amidst great curiosity and expectancy. Shooting was scheduled to begin immediately.

A sizeable portion of the chauffeur's house in Strandhill, adjacent to the castle, was at the team's disposal, and it was in this house that Mr. Padlaski - who appeared to be in charge of accounts - had his office. It was in this house also, in the big bedroom upstairs, next door to Mr Padlaski's office, that my sisters and I had our sleeping accommodation. I worked in the Ashford Industries shop across the yard from the chauffeur's house, and my sisters worked as waitresses in the castle. We all returned to our spacious bedroom when we got off duty each evening.

It was rather unsettling to find our usual night-time tranquillity somewhat disrupted. No one advised us of the new arrangements, and no one provided or suggested a key for our bedroom door either. The house remained open all night as Padlaski and his team came and went with scant regard for time. When the last man left the building all doors remained wide open. No one locked their doors in Ireland, they believed, and they were very happy to go along with that.

The large sitting room downstairs, normally used as a storeroom, was chosen for its size to accommodate Maureen O'Hara's extensive wardrobe where seamstresses stitched torn hems and ironed out creases, working late into the nights to have all costumes ready for the next day's work.

An English chap who dealt with the 'rushes' worked in the pantry from 7pm to midnight, and come what may, Padlaski and his co-workers were pounding up the stairs again at 6am. Sleep was impossible from there on. There was non-stop traffic to the bathroom with queasy tummies for which they apologized profusely, especially when it became obvious that we were to be denied our own morning visit to that all-important little room. Those mornings-after-the-night-before always resulted in numerous trips to the 'wash-room' when Mother Nature beckoned urgently.

"Such wunnerful Irish food and liquor, and now we're belly-aching from over-indulgence," they moaned, while we had assumed, rather naively, that they indulged in nothing but work.

Despite all that, they were a great bunch. They respected our privacy, fully aware that there were three young females sleeping next door. On one of those 'bad' mornings, one of the 'bellyachers' was making a desperate dash for the 'washroom', and in his haste burst open our bedroom door, coming headlong into the middle of the room before he realised his mistake. Muttering 'Gaw-da-amn' under his breath, he retreated hurriedly, while we giggled beneath the bedclothes. Later that day he advised me,

"Get Huggard to buy you a lock for that door, kid. You sure as hell won't always meet nice guys like us."

Obviously, their penchant for unlocked doors did not stretch to young ladies bedrooms.

Rushing indoors from work one evening I noticed that all-important, much talked of wedding dress hanging in the front room awaiting the needlewoman's attention. From that moment onwards the urge to sneak downstairs and fit it on became irresistible. I realised it would prove extremely embarrassing if I were caught in the act, but serve them right for not locking the door, I thought recklessly, when I finally ventured down at 3am while the building was temporarily deserted. I pulled the dress over my head and pirouetted round the room with hammering heart and one eye on the door. It mattered little that it was Maureen O'Hara's wedding dress in the movie. One day, if I should be so fortunate, I, too, might wear a similarly dazzling outfit, I thought dreamily, posturing in front of the mirror, completely oblivious of the bleary eyes and dishevelled hair. Wistfully, I replaced it on its hanger and scampered to the bedroom with just seconds to spare before Padlaski charged up the stairs to his office. It was a close shave. A new dawn broke and I still could not compose myself sufficiently to go back to bed.

Outside in the yard a convoy of trucks containing generators, mobile wardrobes, mobile toilets - in fact everything that was required for the day's shooting - were getting ready to roll at 6.30am. Peeping down from the bedroom window I decided it was a lousy job. Who ever said movie-making was glamorous? You could be forgiven for thinking that these behind-the-scenes hard-working people were indeed the real stars of the show. Acting looked so simple when compared with the hard slog of keeping the show on the road every day.

Film stars were no novelty to these people. They worked with them every day. They had a job to do and worked with incredible speed when time and weather demanded it. Most of them liked to unwind at night with a drink and a chat in the local pubs. That chat revolved mainly around their wives and families back home, particularly if they found a nice sympathetic female who was a good listener.

Working in Ashford Industries shop provided me with an excellent opportunity to talk to all of them when they came to browse 'in your quaint little craft shop'. I, too, became very familiar with their wives likes and dislikes; their children's high-schools; their studies with such strange-sounding names, and their ambitions.

Archie Stout, a brilliant 2nd unit photographer, and a most unassuming man, was one such person. He took a keen interest in our young lives also - our background, our education and our hopes for the future. He took a considerable number of photographs of the staff, myself included, before he returned to his homeland and I feel sure everyone received copies in due course just as I did. On the back of my picture he wrote,

"Think of me sometimes, especially when you see The Quiet Man. Speak to me again in your soft Irish brogue, and then sing for me *'When Irish Eyes Are Smiling'*."

We exchanged letters for a year, towards the end of which his wife became seriously ill with heart problems. He was devastated. The letters dwindled and finally ceased altogether. I never heard of him again.

Script-girl Meta Sterne, who was also director John Ford's girl-Friday, and indeed his right-hand woman, was a homely, friendly lady, obviously determined to shun the limelight at all times. She sat in her chair beside Ford, on location, with the script of the movie on her knees, forever wearing her dark glasses and her huge shady hat. Autograph hunters and snapshot enthusiasts were equally discouraged, so much so that photographs of Meta were - as they say in Cong – 'as scarce as hens' teeth'. She visited the shop the day before she left Ashford Castle and presented me with a copy of the script and asked me to remember her always.

"I guess we will just have our memories," she said thoughtfully, "because it is unlikely that we will ever meet again this side of Kingdom Come."

Prop-man Ace Holmes had his dearest wish granted just hours before he departed for Shannon. Fishing from the riverbank at sundown, he caught 'a beauty of a fish' - albeit a small one - to his everlasting pride and joy, amidst much good-humoured ribbing from his workmates, but Ace couldn't have been happier if he had landed a 30lb salmon.

All too soon their work was finished. They were leaving in droves. The speed of their departure equalled that of their arrival. The clipboard-wielding crew with the important expressions, hollerin' at each other all day were gone forever.

We made many new friends who assured us they would 'mail' us, but they also warned that they were hopeless correspondents, therefore it was no surprise when the promised letters never arrived at the chauffeur's house. Ashford seemed extremely dull and lifeless without them. Even the fact that we had the 'washroom' all to ourselves failed to brighten our mornings.

We missed them more than we cared to admit for a long, long time.

# Anne Morrin

*The Advance Team at work*

CHAPTER 26

# Blow-in From The West

MAY 19TH 1967. A bright sunshiny day with a distinct April feel to it.
The day our world changed when we said farewell to our home in Mayo and opted instead for the midlands, where many families like ourselves were re-located by The Irish Land Commission, in an effort to improve farming conditions for people from the west of Ireland small holding regions. No one was coerced into moving, but people with small scattered farms, especially from Connemara, were greatly encouraged to move to bigger and better farms. For many, it was pure joy to get possession of a holding of land that was all in one piece, rather than in several small divisions as was the custom in the west at that time. The land they left behind was subsequently divided, and as a result, some of the remaining village farmers benefited from the change.

My personal knowledge of migrants going to the midlands was scant indeed. I never for one moment envisaged being one of them. But on that May morning, I wondered many times, how the wives of yesteryear felt on leaving home and family and friends. Did they also feel as I did, torn in two, uncertain, and relying totally on hearsay and intuition that they were making the right decision?

The kids were wildly excited about moving. They were going to have their very own telly for the first time. No more running down to the neighbour's house to watch *Rin-Tin-Tin* and *Lúidín Mac Lúa*. For them it was one great adventure, and the television was the icing on the cake.

Two trucks, one with the cattle and the other with our few bits of furniture and personal belongings, were sent on ahead of us that morning. Sailor, the old collie dog, looked so forlorn and so miserable, not knowing why he was tucked in with bags of grain and turf. For days after we arrived in Mullingar we had to keep him under close observation. He tore down the road with lightning speed at every opportunity, no doubt hitting the road for home, and he was not the only one who was beginning to feel that way .......

We had our lovely brand new house and seventy acres of land, but to our utter dismay we discovered on arrival that we had no electricity and no water. The Land Commission had not, as yet, arranged to have the power switched on for us. For eleven nights we groped around by candlelight when neighbouring migrants came to wish us *céad míle fáilte* and offer some welcome advice on life in the midlands.

We were not quite so fortunate with the water, having to make-do with barrels and buckets for a full year until the next batch of migrants were about to arrive in the village, and wise people that they were, they declined to set foot in the place until such basic necessities as electricity and water were installed.

It was such a let-down. At home in Mayo we had a three hundred gallon tank of water at the back of the house, and one tap in the scullery. Here we had taps all over the place

and they were bone dry. To quote one of the men unloading the trucks,
"They're like tits on a bull, Missus – useless."

It seems incredible now that we relied on going to the lake with two milk churns in a wheel-barrow, to provide water for household use. Tempers were becoming increasingly frayed when, one year later, the new people drove in to the village, and hot on their heels came the most wonderful, welcome sound. The sound of water gushing through the pipes. Water was as precious as gold-dust in that desert-dry never-to-be-forgotten first year.

Despite the bitter frustration we settled in quickly. There was much belated spring-work still to be done, such as potatoes and vegetables waiting to be planted, with little hope of a good crop, but to our delight, the late sowing did not affect the growth in any way.

Fences had to be erected. Meadows had to be taken up. Cows had to be milked and young calves fed. It was a sixteen-hour day, but we still found time to visit our fellow county-men and women, and also found time to have a drink with them on Sunday evenings in Paddy Gallagher's pub, the favourite watering-hole of the west of Ireland crowd.

We were a bit clannish really in those days, preferring to club together. We shared a certain empathy with each other, and whether they hailed from north or south Mayo, or the far-flung corners of Connemara, all seemed to possess that definite something that left us feeling we knew each other intimately all our lives.

We were deeply indebted to our Westmeath neighbours who welcomed us to the county and offered to assist in any way they could. We quickly learned they were not people to push themselves on newcomers. It was up to us to accept their generous offer of help, which we certainly availed of occasionally.

But some of us missed the closeness we had at home in Mayo, where neighbours ran into each others homes at any old time, to borrow 'a grain o'tay or sugar' until the travelling shop called next day......... and that five-minute errand oft times took one hour to accomplish! We missed it, because our next door neighbours were not 'next door' anymore, as houses were well spaced out due to the larger holdings of land acquired by each farmer. Again, we learned something new. Westmeath people did not have the time, nor the inclination to indulge in idle chatter every day. They had their own workload to cope with.

"Well, yez wouldn't have a minit," they told us ruefully, and at first we thought they were a little bit cold, a little bit distant. But, over the years the pattern of our own daily lives became identical, devoting all our time to our families and our farms.

The visits to other migrant homes were spaced out considerably. We made excuses and told ourselves we'd catch up on the visiting when the nights got long. Sadly this never happened. Our kids got their coveted telly and switched on immediately their homework was finished, and gradually, we too, who 'hadn't a minnit' sat down to watch 'the box'.

The chat that we longed for initially was now confined to meeting on the road or in the town, when we renewed the invitations and promises our hearts told us we would not keep, however well-intentioned at the time. We became less dependent on 'our own crowd', having reached the stage when we could purchase a second-hand tractor and third-hand plough or mower, without too much financial strain.

We could now get most of the spring and summer farmwork done without any assistance from others. Every farmer was purchasing more and more farm machinery as time went by, firmly of the opinion that 'there's nothing like having yer own'.

Land Commission advised those of us with low livestock numbers to consider taking out a loan in order to increase our stocking levels. A quantum leap for people who never borrowed anything more than 'the grain o'tay or sugar, or the hayfork', from the neighbours in the old days. Serious lateral thinking was vital before we would allow ourselves to be persuaded by anyone to actually borrow almost one thousand pounds from any financial institution. A daunting prospect indeed. Little did we know then that we had got our first glimpse of the real world where borrowing was the norm everywhere.......... except where we came from.

Integration was simplified by the fact that our children were attending the local primary school. Parents got to know each other through school meetings, collecting their offspring, outdoor activities, etc. The children were exceptionally good mixers, and in turn the parents mixed well also. As a result, we no longer saw ourselves as 'blow-ins', and certainly, Westmeath people no longer thought of us as such.

Thirty-five years on, the number of 'blow-ins' has increased enormously in Westmeath. A gypsy rover once remarked. "If they were all to 'blow out' again, it would be easy to count the natives."

It seems a long time since we left Mayo, and one would expect it to be just a memory, but to quote the herd who worked on the MacCartney estate when we first arrived here,

"The savage loves his native land."

He predicted correctly, that we would always go back, and we HAVE done....... for weddings, funerals, weekending...... any excuse to go 'home' and see them all.

Would we change things if we could turn the clock back?

No. Westmeath has been a good place to live for many reasons. However, each and every one of us has abiding memories of 'home', which are dusted down and polished up with great pleasure and lots of *craic* every time we meet.

*New days, new ways*

ISBN 1425181945-5